Wire till I die
My life in rugby league

Mark Forster
with Gary Slater

London League Publications Ltd

Wire till I die
My life in rugby league
Mark Forster with Gary Slater

© Mark Forster and Gary Slater. Foreword © Lee Briers. Introduction © Gary Slater.

The moral right of Mark Forster and Gary Slater to be identified as the authors has been asserted.

Cover design © Stephen McCarthy.

Cover photos: Front: Mark Forster makes a break in November 1987 (Photo: Eddie Fuller), Mark gets his breath back after a superb length–of–the–field try for Ireland against New Zealand Maori in the 2000 Rugby League World Cup (Photo: Mike Boden, *Warrington Guardian*), Mark scoring against Dewsbury at Wilderspool in April 1986 (Photo: Eddie Whitham). Back: the 1990 Warrington team that reached the Challenge Cup Final (Photo: Eddie Whitham).

All photographs are as credited to the photographer or provider of the photo. No copyright has been intentionally breached; please contact London League Publications Ltd if you believe there has been a breach of copyright.

A CIP catalogue record for this book is available from the British Library.

First published in Great Britain in April 2016 by London League Publications Ltd,
PO Box 65784, London NW2 9NS

ISBN: 978-1-909885-10-3

Cover design by Stephen McCarthy Graphic Design, 46, Clarence Road, London N15 5BB

Editing and layout by Peter Lush

Printed and bound in Great Britain by Charlesworth Press, Wakefield

Foreword

I remember the very first time I spoke to Foz. I had just signed for Warrington from St Helens, aged 18, in the board room at Wilderspool on a Friday in April 1997. The team were preparing to play Saints at Knowsley Road on the Sunday. Darryl van de Velde, the Warrington coach, said: "Welcome to the team. Go and get your kit. You are playing at the weekend."

I walked into the video room and Foz stood up and said: "If you don't need your complimentary tickets for the weekend, I'll have them." He was being a bit tongue in cheek because, as a St Helens lad, I was definitely going to use my tickets. That was the first time I had met him and from that minute onwards we clicked and have been great friends ever since.

I was ready to go out and spend the money I had got for signing but, after that first conversation about the tickets, the second one was "Look after your money and make sure your future is sorted. Buy property because your career will be over before you know it" – and he was right.

I have been told that Foz and I are the only two players alive who have made more than 400 appearances for Warrington and that gives me goose bumps. Warrington is a special club and has had some special players and to be in that category – just Mark and me – is fantastic.

He was the original home-grown legend. He was Mr Warrington. He gave everything for the club. He was as tough as nails and I mean that with the highest regard because he wasn't a dirty player. For a winger, he was very tough and he had the great ability to score fantastic tries. His record speaks for itself.

When I started at Warrington, Foz was 32 and coming towards the end of his career and gave great advice. I would like to think that I took some of his leadership into my late career and that when I was 32, 33 and 34 I gave good advice to youngsters.

I remember his 400th game, against Bradford, when he was presented with his golden boots and scored a couple of tries in a famous victory. It was a great occasion. That is something special and something to look back on with pride. I can't speak highly enough of him. Not only was he a good team-mate, but he was a top bloke off the field and used to look after us. Foz and his wife Gaynor looked after me and my partner Vicky. We were only young; Gaynor was like our second mum and Foz was like our second dad. Foz's door was open to everybody.

I also played against him once for Wales versus Ireland in Swansea, but I made sure I stayed away from his right arm, his swinging arm. I think he is mental to still be playing as an amateur at the age of 50, but that's Foz. He loves the competition, the camaraderie and the social side of the game, which you do miss. As long as his body is willing, why not?

Lee Briers
October 2015

Introduction

Mark Forster played for Ireland in the 2000 Rugby League World Cup, scored a try on his Great Britain debut, won three caps for the Great Britain under-21s, represented Lancashire and had a season with Widnes Vikings in the Northern Ford Premiership. He was also crowned the fastest man in rugby league. But he will always be best remembered for his extraordinary career with Warrington Wolves. No man alive has made more than his 458 appearances for the club. Of the current squad, Ben Westwood is closest. By the end of 2015 he had made 364 appearances for Warrington – still 94 (or three good years) behind.

For an incredible 19 seasons, Foz featured on the wing – left or right –and ran in try after try after try. His final tally of 191 leaves him in fourth place in the club's all-time list behind world record holder Brian Bevan (740), the legendary Jack Fish (214) and Welsh powerhouse John Bevan (201).

Like all great wingers, Foz was blessed with pace but he also had courage, strength, a phenomenal work ethic, a rugby brain and another attribute that earned him the respect of Warrington fans: he was a local lad, he was one of them. Born and bred in the town, Foz was a Warrington supporter before he was a Warrington player and continues to be a fan to this day. Wire till I die, you might say.

Of all the tries that Foz scored, the one he is most proud of came in the 1990 Challenge Cup semi-final against Oldham at Central Park. It was a routine winger's try, Foz caught a peach of a pass and touched down in the corner. He scored dozens like it in his career, but this one was special because it took his beloved Warrington back to Wembley after a gap of 15 years – far too long for a club of the history, standing and potential of Warrington.

Like every rugby player, Foz suffered some cruel injuries – including a dislocated shoulder in that Wembley Final and two broken arms – but the most painful blow he suffered in his two decades at Wilderspool was when he was released by coach Darryl van de Velde in late 2000. He never pulled on a Warrington shirt again in a competitive match. Foz had just turned 35, but felt he was good enough, fit enough and hungry enough for another season in Super League, another year in which he could have scored his 200th try for Warrington. That was not to be, although he did notch up the 200th try of his career during his swansong season at Widnes, a campaign that ended with the Vikings being promoted to Super League for the first time.

Yet Foz's professional career is only half of the story. Before joining Warrington he was an outstanding junior player, representing his school, his town, the North West Counties and England Schoolboys, alongside the likes of Shaun Wane and Garry Schofield. After leaving Widnes, he returned to the amateur ranks with great success with Rylands Sharks, Bank Quay Bulls and Woolston Rovers. He celebrated his 50th birthday in November 2014 but is still playing regularly – often in the same side as his sons Chris and Dan. Rugby league is the family business, with wife Gaynor, daughter Beckie and grandchildren Taylor and Maisie cheering on from the touchlines.

One of the enduring strengths of Wigan Warriors has been the seemingly never-ending production line of local talent the town supplies for the team. Warrington Wolves have not been so fortunate, but in Mark Forster they had a player who did just about everything there was to achieve in the game. It has been an honour and a privilege to tell his story.

Gary Slater
January 2016

Good times and bad times

While writing this book a big part of my family's life has been sadly taken away from us all – my father-in-law Colin (CJ) Jordan. He went everywhere with his daughter Gaynor following me, following his grandsons and, later on in life, his great grandson. He will be sadly missed by all.

Plus I want to give a massive thanks to Gaynor, Christopher, Daniel, Beckie, Taylor and Maisie for keeping me going through good times and bad times. Massive thanks also to my mum and dad and to everybody who has contributed to this book. I hope it's a good read.

Mark Forster
February 2016

Thank you

The authors would like to thank the *Warrington Guardian* and, in particular sports editor Mike Parsons, chief photographer Mike Boden and former chief photographer Eddie Fuller, for their help and support over an extended period – more than 30 years. They would also like to thank another photographer, Eddie Whitham, for his excellent contributions. Thanks are also due to Gary Skentelbery of *Warrington Worldwide* for his picture of the 1991 Regal Trophy-winning team. Special thanks also to Ken and Doreen Forster, Mark's mum and dad, for their help with family photographs and long-treasured newspaper cuttings.

London League Publications Ltd would like to thank Steve McCarthy for designing the cover and the staff of Charlesworth Press for printing the book.

About Gary Slater

Gary Slater is a former deputy sports editor of the *Warrington Guardian* and, since 1996, has been a sports journalist with *The Daily Telegraph* in London. He is married to Helen and has four sons – Joe, Tom, Ben and Jack – and one grandson, Zack. They all support Warrington Wolves. They have to. In 2014, he helped Warrington legend Mike Nicholas write his acclaimed autobiography *From Swn-y-mor to Seattle – Nicko's rugby odyssey*.

Other books by Gary Slater:

With Tempus Publishing/the History Press:
Warrington Rugby League Club 1970-2000, Images of Sport (2000)
Warrington Rugby League Club, 100 Greats (2002)
(both with Eddie Fuller)
The Official Warrington Wolves Miscellany (2012)

With London League Publications Ltd:
So close to Glory, Warrington Rugby League Club 1919-39 (2008) (With Eddie Fuller)
Jack Fish, A rugby league superstar (2012)
From Swn-y-Mor to Seattle, Nicko's rugby odyssey (2014) (With Mike Nicholas)

Mark with the Ernie Ashcroft Shield as man-of-the-match in the 1989 Locker Cup match.
(Photo: Eddie Fuller)

Contents

MARK FORSTER
TESTIMONIAL 1992

The brochure from Mark's first testimonial year with Warrington.
(Courtesy Gary Slater)

1. Hurly-burly with Norman Turley

Warrington 'A' 30 Rochdale Hornets 'A' 14
Friday, 16 October 1981, Lancashire Combination

This was my first trial game for Warrington and our coach Tony Barrow had a "one in, all in" mentality if there was any trouble because, he said, the referee couldn't send all 13 players off. I was a young lad, still at Richard Fairclough High School and aged only 16. I was playing centre. Tony said: "It's OK Mark. You will be all right today. I have got an experienced winger looking after you in Rick Thackray." Rick had already made 50 appearances for the first team and won the Lancashire Cup and the John Player Trophy.

Anyway, there was a brawl and it kicked off just outside the dugouts where Tony Barrow was sitting. So I thought: "I'm going to have to get stuck in here." I got stuck in, but Rick walked away back to his wing, not doing anything, and I was left fighting with the former Warrington player Norman Turley, who was about six feet three inches and 15 stones, and I was five feet 10 inches and skinny. We beat the living daylights out of each other for a while and the referee sent me off. I thought that was my Warrington career over before it had even started. I sat in the dressing room, threw my boots across the room and had a bit of a tantrum.

Then I heard the clicking of boots in the tunnel and heard the dressing room door start to open. I was a bit worried in case it was Norman Turley, looking for me, but it was our hooker, Tommy Cunningham. "It's all right, Foz," he said: "I got him back for you." He had obviously had a go at Norman and been sent off as well. Two Rochdale players were sent off too and our centre, Ronnie Duane, went off at half-time with a broken thumb. It was an eventful debut.

In the bar after the match I felt a tap on my shoulder. I turned round and it was Norman Turley offering to buy me a pint. I said I'd just have an orange and lemonade thanks. "No," he said. "Have a pint." "I can't Norman," I told him. "I'm only 16." "Bloody hell," said Norman. "Please don't tell anyone I was having a fight with a 16-year-old." He was 26 at the time. Sorry, Norman, your secret's out.

I was suspended for one match for that fight and Tommy Cunningham was suspended for two. Thankfully, Warrington still wanted to sign me. In fact, Tony Barrow – the very, very loud Tony Barrow – told my mum and dad that I wasn't signing for anyone else but Warrington. If I didn't sign for Warrington, he would break my legs. Luckily, my mum and dad found that quite funny. They also said the living room was still ringing for two hours after he finished talking because he was so loud. I signed as a wannabe loose-forward and goalkicker but, in 20 years, I never actually played as a loose-forward in the first team and I only kicked three goals. However, I did score a few tries.

Warrington's 'A' team did the Lancashire Combination and Lancashire Shield double in the 1981–82 season. Left to right, back: Tony Barrow (coach), Steve Moylan, Gary Dainty, Paul Fellows, Mark Gleave, Mark Forster, Ian Duane, Peter Turner, John Peake; kneeling: Tommy Rawlinson, Billy Cowell, Alan Gwilliam, Derek Finnigan, Kenny Paget, Paul Ford, Derek Whitehead (trainer). (Photo: Eddie Fuller).

I played hooker in a training match once. It was Tony Barrow's bright idea to have the first team against the 'A' team at Wilderspool and the coaches played as well so that they could see what was going on at close quarters. I remember running down the leisure centre side of the ground towards the Fletcher Street End. I took on Derek Whitehead, the assistant coach, on the outside. He had been a brilliant full-back in the 1970s, but still had a little bit of pace and tapped my ankles. I went down, fell on my elbow and dislocated my shoulder. Derek and I still laugh about that now, Derek more than me obviously.

Dr Rothwell, the club doctor, tried to put the shoulder back in but couldn't and I was screaming the place down. He was a cracking doctor. I remember in one match having a clash of heads at the Railway End, where the big blue gates were. There was a lot of blood, but this was before they introduced the blood bin. I finished the set of six tackles and was substituted and ran down the tunnel. Dr Rothwell was already there, threading the needle and said "I'll have you back on in five minutes". He kept his word.

I signed for Warrington on a Friday afternoon outside Ockher's house in Fletcher Street. Ockher – aka Roy Aspinall – was the groundsman and he became a great friend of mine, even though he took a lot of money off me at cards and made me buy my own kit and things like that. If you asked him for a pair of laces or a jockstrap or towel, he would have it written down in his book when you last had one and if it wasn't long enough you

2

wouldn't get another one. Even if yours had been stolen or your boots had split, if it wasn't long enough, you weren't getting them. Warrington wanted me to play for the 'A' team against Barrow that night and I signed on the bonnet of one of the directors' cars, a Jaguar, while the team were watching. I said to the lads: "They're not bad club cars are they?" All the lads were wound up, thinking that I had got a Jaguar as a club car, but I didn't even have a driving licence at the time.

I have still got my copy of the contract – signed by myself and Graham McCarty, Warrington's general manager – which promised me £12,000 for relinquishing my amateur status. The signing-on fee was £3,000 – cash – with the rest to be paid in instalments: £1,000 on my 18th birthday, £1,500 on my 19th, £1,500 on my 20th birthday, £1,000 after playing for Lancashire, £2,000 after playing for Great Britain and a final £2,000 after going on tour with Great Britain to Australia or New Zealand. It sounds a lot, but our wages were only £25 a win in the 'A' team and £100 a win in the first team. Tax was taken out of that and we were all part-time.

My signing present was a Barrow loose-forward called Eddie Szymala. He liked the gym. He was the biggest thing I had ever seen. I was still at school. I scooted straight from the base of a scrum and there he was, looking like Popeye, with enormous arms. His arms were as big as my legs and he didn't miss. After that I soon learned to run a bit wider from the scrum. We always used to have a winger taking the ball in straight from the scrum and it went on for years and years. Even when the likes of Tawera Nikau and Brendon Tuuta were playing at Castleford, Ellery Hanley at Wigan and Lee Crooks at Hull, they used to wait at the base of the scrum and smash the Warrington winger. When I got into the Great Britain camp they would say "Foz, why do you always run the ball in? Every loose-forward in rugby league knows" – and this was before videos and DVDs – "that you or the other winger is going to drive it in from the scrum." I said that was what Kevin Ashcroft and Tony Barrow told us to do and we just did what we were told. Great Britain decided to do it as well. I said to Lee Crooks he had just told me it was a waste of time. "Yes," he said. "But you're taking one of our drives in for us forwards, so that's different." But that was all in the future. We got our win against Barrow and I got my £25 winning pay and the following Monday I was the richest boy in school.

After that, when the teacher asked everyone in English what they did on Friday night and what they did at the weekend I used to tell them all the stories about playing for Warrington and elaborate a little bit about going night-clubbing with all the first team players. I never got an 'A', I always got a 'B+'. Even the teacher didn't believe me.

We had a PE teacher called Colin Meachin who played for Salford. PE was the last lesson on a Friday. One Friday night Warrington 'A' were playing Salford 'A' and another of the PE teachers, Steve Howson, found out we would be playing against each other. During the lesson, Mr Meachin kicked the ball down the middle of the field and said: "I'll chase you for that." I got there first and he tackled me quite hard. I said: "You won't catch me tonight either." But, during the match, I caught him. Just before I tackled him I said: "I am going to get you sir." One of his team-mates shouted: "Foz, you're not one of his pupils are you?" I said I was and they gave him a load of stick because one of his pupils had caught him. Mr Meachin didn't like it, of course, and said: "You're in detention on Monday."

Warrington's 'A' team did the double that season, 1981–82, winning the Lancashire Combination and the Lancashire Shield, beating Whitehaven 'A' in both legs of the final. The 'A' team was made up of some players with lots of first team experience, such as scrum-half Alan Gwilliam, centre Ian Duane and full-back Derek Finnigan, young players learning their trade, such as myself, hooker Steve Moylan and winger Paul Fellows, and another winger named Billy Cowell. Known to one and all as 'Billy Whizz', Billy never played for the first team, but joined the backroom staff and was a great friend to all of us and Warrington through and through. Sadly, like Ockher, he is no longer with us. We paraded both trophies around the ground before the first team match against Barrow. Four days later – at lunchtime on Thursday, 29 April – the main stand burnt down.

I was at Warrington Collegiate at the time, I did one day and one night a week there as part of my joinery apprenticeship, and one of the lads had a car. We could see the smoke from the other side of town, but nobody knew where it was coming from. So we jumped in the car, followed the smoke and ended up behind the back of the Wilderspool Leisure Centre, watching in disbelief as the stand burnt to the ground.

Soon after that I started working for one of Warrington's sponsors, Ashalls Construction, and they got the contract to build the new stand, the Brian Bevan Stand. Four Warrington players worked as joiners or apprentice joiners for the company – John Fieldhouse, Ronnie and Ian Duane and myself – and if we were lucky enough to get Saturday morning overtime we would hop over the fence for training, get changed, train and then hop over the fence again to finish the shift off. A lot of the builders on the site used to stop work and watch us train. It was a real privilege to help build that stand.

We all ended up as qualified joiners. John Fieldhouse came as a qualified joiner while Ian and Ronnie Duane started their apprenticeships there and I finished my apprenticeship there. When Ronnie went to Australia on the 1984 Great Britain tour – more of that later – he was presented with a gold carriage clock by Jack Ashall to mark his achievement. When I went to Australia the following summer to play for Brisbane Norths – more of that later too – I was given my cards. They told me not to come back. They said they had had enough of rugby players – they kept getting injured or going on tour – and wouldn't be employing any more. Ian liked to think he was the best and neatest joiner but Ronnie, John and myself all went on to play for Great Britain and he didn't so we'll give him that.

2. Wembley ballboy

I was born Mark James Forster in Warrington Maternity Home at Victoria Park on 25 November 1964. My dad Ken was a steel fixer. He worked on building sites all over the place, which is similar to what I do now. My mum Doreen used to work in the local offices of Firth Wire, a wiredrawing company, which is the industry where the Wire get their nickname from. We lived in a two-up, two-down in Wellington Street in Howley, with my sister Dawn, who was a year older than me. She was very posh and went to an all-girls school, Warrington High School for Girls. I went to the local Richard Fairclough High School, the rag and bone, the down and out school. She was the clever one, she had the brains, and I'm not sure what I got.

Wellington Street was just a walk over Victoria Park to school, although nine times out of 10 it was a run because I was always late. I am still always late to this day. If we are going out for the night at 7.30pm, they tell me it's 7.15pm and I'm still five minutes late. I am renowned for it. I ended up running to school most days and if the River Mersey flooded, like it used to do, I used to be even later because I had to run around the flood. People tell me I will be late for my own funeral. But I think all this sprinting to get into school before they closed the doors made me a faster runner. That's my excuse anyway.

On the way home, after I had stopped behind to play sport or do detention, I used to see the Warrington team training in the park and I thought to myself: "One day, I'll give that a go." I had a few training sessions with Latchford Albion, but I had a mate who was playing for Woolston Rovers and he asked me if I wanted to go down there. Brian Chambers was coaching at Latchford and he took me to Woolston, who had a better junior set-up at the time. I was 12 years old. That's Brian's claim to fame: that he discovered Mark Forster. He keeps telling my mum now that I should retire because I am making him feel old.

After I had been playing for Woolston for a couple of seasons, Jackie Melling, the former Warrington and Wigan centre, came to see me and asked if I would sign for Wigan St Patrick's. They had players like Mike Gregory, Andy Platt and Joe Lydon. They would get me to training twice a week, on Tuesday and Thursday nights. All my parents had to do was pick me up. My mum and dad said it was up to me, but they were both working full-time and I decided it wouldn't be fair on them to have to collect me every Tuesday and Thursday. So I stayed with Woolston. Who knows? I might have got lost at St Pat's. Instead of being a big fish in a small pond at Woolston, I would have been a small fish in a big pond at St Pat's. But even at that stage, Warrington were showing an interest in me and so I stayed loyal to Woolston.

From seeing the Warrington players training on the park, my heroes like Ken Kelly, Dave Chisnall and John Bevan, to actually getting changed next to them and playing with them was only about five years. I did three years at Woolston, coached by Brian Chambers, and then Albert "Snowy" Rowlands, the Warrington scout, asked three of us – Paul Bing, Keith

Thomason and myself – to start training with Warrington. Paul and Keith were forwards and had started working. They could only make training every now and again and fell by the wayside. I was still at school, which finished at 4pm, and so I could always make training.

I went to my first function as a Warrington player in September 1981. It was at the Parr Hall and was a *Sunday Mirror* Roadshow for Parry Gordon's second testimonial season. The show was hosted by the broadcaster Keith Macklin and presented by David Howes, the RFL's public relations officer, with John Huxley of the *Sunday Mirror*. Mick Morgan, of Featherstone Rovers, was the auctioneer. It was good to be seen with the likes of Parry, Derek Finnigan, Eddie Hunter and Ronnie and Ian Duane and I got my picture in the *Warrington Guardian*. Parry was a hero of mine and a legend in Warrington. I never played with him for the first team, but I did a lot of training with him. He was a great player. Half-backs take some stick now but at least they have a little bit of muscle. I looked at Parry, all skin and bone, and wondered how he survived the tackles he made and the forwards running at him.

Long before then I used to watch Warrington with my granddad, Ernest Jennings, and my uncle, Curtis Jennings. My dad would only really go to finals, he wasn't that into it, but we all went to Wembley against Featherstone in 1974. I was only nine and I remember sitting on the barriers. We all went again the following year against Widnes and I remember sitting on the front row of the old wooden stand at Wilderspool when they beat Australia in 1978. I wasn't quite old enough to play in that one because I was only 13. I was a young outside back and a wannabe loose-forward and I always looked up to full-back Derek Finnigan, who was an old head, but my main hero was John Bevan.

Derek gave me a bit of advice when I signed for Warrington: don't hang around at one club for too long. I said: "OK Derek, I won't." Twenty years later, we were at a sportsman's dinner together with the past players and he came over to me and said: "What did I tell you?" I said: "I know, but I've never listened to anybody." Later on, John Woods gave me similar advice after he had spent 10 years at Leigh. But loyalty does have its rewards. Last year, I did a charity bike ride to help raise money for a statue of John to be erected at Leigh Sports Village. Jason Donohue, Leigh's general manager, rang me up and I was only too happy to help.

As a lad I did a paper round, even though I was always late, and I remember we did two rounds on a Friday because we had the big *Warrington Guardians* to deliver as well. I also joined the choir at Warrington Parish Church, which was a bit daunting until they told me I would get paid 15p a week for doing it. And if we did a wedding on a Saturday we got an extra 25p. So I would do the Sunday morning service and sing in the choir, go to watch Warrington play in the afternoon and go back to church for Evensong, carrying my Warrington programme. I would sing the hymns, but when the priest started giving his sermon I would read the programme – until he spotted me and banned me from taking my programmes to church. But I think I have been forgiven because I got married there and my three children were christened there.

Wembley ballboys 1978. Left to right: Chris Hough (Beamont), David Hill (English Martyrs), Brian Paget (Beamont), Ian Charnock and Mark Forster (both Richard Fairclough), John Gordon (Beamont), David Johnson (English Martyrs), Paul Barker (Beamont), Bill Withington (Bewsey), Colin Kelly (Beamont), coach Keith Jones and Warrington League secretary Walter Norris. (Photo: *Warrington Guardian*).

I really got interested in sport in my early days at Richard Fairclough High School. I was into football, I was into rugby and I played basketball. At football, I played centre-forward because of my speed and we went on tour to Belgium. My team-mates would kick the ball over the top and I would chase it and hopefully score. It was a bit like playing with Jonathan Davies years later. Two of us – Ian Charnock and I – were the kings of sport. He emigrated to Canada and became a multi-millionaire with a cleaning business. I'm still in Warrington and not a multi-millionaire.

Ian and I both played rugby league for the school team and the town team, Warrington Schoolboys, and in May 1978 we both went to Wembley to be ballboys at the Challenge Cup final between Leeds and St Helens. Ten Warrington schoolboys from the under–13s team were chosen and we had our picture on the front page of the *Warrington Guardian* with our coach, Keith Jones, and Walter Norris, who was the secretary of the Warrington League. The other eight ballboys were Chris Hough, Brian Paget, John Gordon, Paul Barker and Colin Kelly, from Beamont School, David Hill and David Johnson, from English Martyrs, and Bill Withington, from Bewsey. We travelled to London the day before the final and stayed in a hotel, in pairs, on the Friday night. Chris Hough and Brian Paget were sharing a room and a huge mirror on the back of their bedroom door fell off and smashed.

Top: A young Mark on a family holiday in Newquay, Cornwall in the 1960s.
Middle: On holiday in Cornwall in 1967 with mum, dad, uncle Curtis Jennings and granddad Ernest Jennings.

Bottom: Mark with his sister, Dawn. He says that she got all the brains. (Photos: courtesy Forster family).

Mark's parents, Ken and Doreen Forster, have celebrated their golden wedding anniversary.

Choirboy Mark on left, with his cousins Peter Miller, Andrew Miller, Robert Miller and sister Dawn outside Warrington Town Hall following a Warrington Walking Day in the early 1970s. (Photos: courtesy Forster family).

They were worried they wouldn't be allowed to go to the final. After breakfast we played tick-and-pass in the hotel car park with some of the other guests before leaving for Wembley. We arrived very early and were allowed to explore. So we sat in the Queen's seat in the Royal Box and walked up the 39 steps and pretended to collect the trophy. When we finally walked out of the tunnel with the teams the atmosphere was electric. I remember I was on duty behind the posts when one of the St Helens players, it might have been Derek Noonan, attempted a drop-goal. It was heading my way and I was worried that I would drop the ball in front of a crowd of 95,872 and millions more watching on television.

Thankfully, the ball hit the post and bounced back into play. One of my Warrington heroes, Dave Chisnall, was in the St Helens team. Leeds won a classic final 14–12 despite George Nicholls, the St Helens second row, winning the Lance Todd Trophy as man-of-the-match. After the final hooter sounded we all ran on to the pitch and tried to jump in front of the cameras. It was a trip we would never forget. Brian has still got the official tracksuit top we were issued on the day – and I bet he's not the only one.

I never missed a day at school and used to get certificates for 100 per cent attendance. If I was going to be off for some reason I just used to say I was going to represent the school at sport and they used to mark me in. Whenever I got into trouble, which was very rarely, I had to go and see the head teacher, Mr Baker. If he looked like he was going for the cane drawer or the ruler, I used to talk about sport and slowly turn him around. He would ask: "What have you represented the school at this weekend?" And I would say cross-country or football or basketball or rugby. He would say: "We'll let this one go this time." I must have got away with things a dozen times like that. I wasn't an angel at school, but I was quick at getting away from the teachers. They caught the slower ones and I got away with it. In my fourth-year report Mr Baker wrote that I would never make a living out of rugby league and woodwork, but I have been pretty successful in both, so that just shows what he knew.

I was always being dragged up in front of the full school assembly every single Friday to say "Mark Forster's doing this, Mark Forster's doing that". I played for North West Counties Schools against France when I was 16. I had to go to Oldham to train. The school paid for a teacher to take me over and bought me a full kit, brand new boots, Patrick Kevin Keegan boots, black with a green stripe, and a brand new tracksuit. Mr Baker got me up again in front of the full assembly to present them and the whole school had to applaud me, which was all right until dinner time when all the lads wanted to take the mickey out of me for being a teachers' pet.

North West Counties Schools 13 France under–16s 13
Monday 6 April 1981
Luckily enough, the match was played at Wilderspool. It was the first time I had played a proper match there and I loved every minute of it. It made me want to play there again and again and again. Another Warrington lad, John Gordon, from Beamont School, was in

10

the North West Counties team. Surprise, surprise, his nickname was Flash after Flash Gordon and he was fast as well. He played for Crosfields. I was at centre and he was my winger. I still see him in Warrington, although he is not involved in rugby anymore.

Four days after facing France at Wilderspool I played against them again when I made my debut for England Schoolboys at Widnes's Naughton Park. The French schoolboys, as usual, had beards and drove their own cars to the ground and gave out a bit of stick. Luckily, one of the touch judges was Mike Loftus from Warrington. One of the French lads was running through and I caught Mike's eye and he nodded and I gave the French lad the biggest hit I could, and another one on the way down and landed on the back of his head with my arm. Mike just looked away and the French lad was flat out. The French referee asked him: "What happened there?" Mike said: "I didn't see it." I met him two years later in a local sports club and he said: "You owe me a pint." And I said: "What for?" He said: "That French lad. I saw every bit of it. You owe me a pint."

I remember that we all had to wear black boots with brand new white laces, pure white laces, unwrapped that day, so that we all looked smart and looked the same. Before kick-off we were introduced to the Mayor of Halton, they played the national anthems and we lost 12–8. Looking at the team photograph now, I am kneeling next to a young and fresh-faced Garry Schofield, from Hunslet, who was only a substitute that day. A young and fresh-faced Deryck Fox was captain, and a young and fresh-faced David Creasser played. In fact, we were all young and fresh-faced, even Andy Dannatt and Shaun Wane who went on to become big, ugly props.   The full England team was: Phil Pendlebury (Wigan), Gary Clark (Hull), David Creasser (Hunslet), Nick Marner (Oldham), Mark Forster, Deryck Fox (Dewsbury), Tony Collinson (Hull), Chris Swann (Wigan), Neil Puckering (Hull), Shaun Wane (Wigan), Andy Dannatt (Hull), Jeff Clare (Wigan) and Mark Ragan (Hunslet); Subs: Garry Schofield (Hunslet), Simon Leary (Hunslet), David Hatch (Wigan), Wayne Baldwinson (Hunslet). We were coached by Dennis McHugh from Wigan.

I left school at 16 with five 'O' Levels. My mum was amazed that I got so many. She thought there had been a misprint. But I had had enough of school by the time I was 14 to be honest. Like a lot of lads, I wanted to be a mechanic and mess about with cars. I went to the Job Centre and ended up with a job as a labourer with Wallace Construction in Penketh, which turned very quickly into a job as an apprentice joiner. Tom Wallace took six labourers on and there were three apprenticeships available: for a joiner, a plumber and a bricklayer. I was there for 18 months, until halfway through my apprenticeship.

Photo: Shaking hands before the kick-off. (Photo: courtesy Forster family)

11

England Schoolboys versus France at Naughton Park in April 1981. The team was: Phil Pendlebury (Wigan); Gary Clark (Hull), David Creasser (Hunslet), Nick Marner (Oldham), Mark Forster (Warrington); Deryck Fox (Dewsbury), Tony Collinson (Hull); Chris Swann (Wigan), Neil Puckering (Hull), Shaun Wane (Wigan), Andy Dannatt (Hull), Jeff Clare (Wigan), Mark Ragan (Hunslet). Subs: Garry Schofield (Hunslet), Simon Leary (Hunslet), David Hatch (Wigan), Wayne Baldwinson (Hunslet). Coach: Dennis McHugh (Wigan).

The two teams line up for the national anthems. (Both photos: courtesy Forster family)

3. Warrington debut

I was hoping to make my first team debut against Leeds, the league leaders, at Wilderspool on Sunday 9 January 1983. I was the substitute back and the late Dave Chisnall was the substitute forward. Chissie was another great from the 1970s. He had phenomenal speed for a big man and his hands were unbelievable, but neither of us left the bench as Warrington lost 13–12. It was frustrating but I only had to wait another week.

Barrow 17 Warrington 10
Sunday, 16 January 1983, Slalom Lager Championship
So I made my debut in this match instead – aged 18 – and it has gone down in Warrington history, although that was nothing to do with me. Chissie was again on the substitutes' bench, but this time he got on the pitch at the start of the second half and flattened Ron O'Regan with a high tackle to become the first Warrington player to be sent to the sin bin. An old lady hit Chissie with her umbrella as he walked off the pitch. Neil Courtney, the Warrington prop, and David Cairns, the Barrow scrum-half, had already been sent off for fighting and Neil had been warned twice before that. I played centre to Rick Thackray who had 'looked after' me so well in my first trial match, but we both managed to keep out of trouble. Bob Eccles and Phil Ford scored the Warrington tries and Steve 'The Boot' Hesford kicked two goals.

Kevin Ashcroft was the Warrington coach at the time and he knew everything about the game. He knew all the niggles and about pinching players on the back of their arms and legs. We would get a slap, a punch or a headbutt because it is one of those things that really hurts and niggles people. We got a good hiding but got a penalty and the ball back. It was about winding the opposition up. It was mind games.

I remember going to Oldham once and they had painted the away dressing room ceiling pink with lemon stripes and there was just one 40 watt light bulb. Roby Muller, our Kiwi forward, said it had been done to relax us so that we weren't fired up when we went out on the field. Ockher was forever taking light bulbs out of the away dressing room at Wilderspool, or flooding the dressing room, or leaving them with no toilet roll or turning the water off.

Kevin Ashcroft shared all his knowledge of the game with everybody. When we are talking now at sportsman's dinners or other events he always says it was one of his best decisions to give me my debut – even if it was a week late. So that's another one taking credit. I mustn't have done anything on my own!

Hull Kingston Rovers 9 Warrington 9
Sunday, 10 April 1983, Slalom Lager Championship
I scored my first try in this one, when tries were only worth three points. Loose-forward Carl Webb was tackled just short of the line and I dived over. Tries went up to four points

at the start of the next season. Fifteen years later, when I was still in the first team and still scoring tries, the fact I had scored a three-point try was regularly trotted out to show how old I was. Bloody journalists.

It was bitterly cold and snowy and the fans were so close to the pitch that we were getting bombarded with snowballs. John Bevan was my centre and he turned round and shouted at me: "Foz, concentrate on your game and stop throwing snowballs at me." I replied: "John, it's the speccies." Next thing John looked over and a snowball hit him on the side of the head. I said to him: "I told you it wasn't me."

A Maori called Wayne Poutama made his one and only appearance for the first team in this match, at full-back. He had arrived at Warrington the previous October with Roby Muller. The story goes that Warrington had actually signed his brother, Warren Poutama, but he broke his arm and so his brother came instead for a holiday. Warren was, apparently, a good player, but Wayne weighed 10 stones and seemed to be scared of his own shadow. He got hypothermia and came off at half-time. He was a strange shade of blue. The medical staff had to lower him carefully into a bath of warm water to bring his body temperature back up to normal.

Warrington were suffering from an injury crisis at the time and so nine of us who played away to Hull KR had to play for the 'A' team at St Helens in the first leg of the Lancashire Shield Final the next day. Amazingly, the score was 0–0 at half-time and we were only trailing 5–2 with five minutes left before losing 13–2. We were knackered. The second leg was played at Wilderspool on a Sunday morning with an 11am kick-off and we had our photograph taken beforehand. We won 9–3 with an Ian Duane try and three goals from Paul Ford, but it was not quite enough and we lost the final 16–11 on aggregate.

That summer I was lucky enough to play in John Bevan's two testimonial matches. For the one at Wilderspool, I was a substitute, one of the "A. N. Others" and was really proud of that. I thought "If I don't go any further in rugby league, at least I have played in my hero's testimonial match." I also went to the Rhondda Valley for John's second testimonial game and scored a try. When I signed for Warrington I was playing open age and for the Under–19s at Woolston, but Warrington made me join Crosfields because they had an Under–17s team. It was the only one in town. So the Woolston people say I signed for Warrington from them, but the Crosfields committee say my last game before playing for Warrington was for them. They are both right, but if I had to pick a club I would say Woolston because they looked after me as a young lad and took me all the way through. I plan to retire from playing there as well.

I went to the Rhondda Valley game on a double decker bus from Crosfields. It was the scene of one of Mike Nicholas's famous sendings-off, Ian Duane broke his arm, somebody else broke a leg and somebody else broke a jaw. By the time the game and the presentations had finished and we had had our food and drink, it seemed like the whole of the Rhondda Valley had come out to beat the s..t out of us down the main street. There were about 50 of us and I just stood at the back and let it happen. I learnt early on to keep my head down and do as I'm told when I'm told.

Warrington's 'A' team before the Lancashire Shield final, second leg, against St Helens at Wilderspool, April 1983. Left to right, back row: Tony Barrow (coach), Gary Dainty, Mike Gregory, Carl Webb, Mark Gleave, Ian Duane, Mark Forster, Paul Fellows, Alan Scott, Derek Whitehead (Asst coach), Billy 'Whizz' Cowell (trainer); front: Peter Halpin, Tommy Rawlinson, Brian Carbert, Wayne Poutama, Paul Ford, Steve Morris, Steve Moylan, John Round.

Warrington team at Blackpool Borough Lancashire Cup first round, September 1983. Left to right, back: Ronnie Duane, Tony Worrall, Mike Gregory, Bob Eccles, Steve Hesford, Dave Chisnall, Mal Yates. Front: Derek Finnigan, Ken Kelly (captain), John Bevan, Roger O'Mahony, Mark Forster, Paul Cullen. Subs: (not pictured) Alan Scott and Billy McGinty. (Both photos: Eddie Fuller)

There was an aura about Mike Nicholas. Towards the end of his career he was never the best trainer because his knees were so sore. I was at a match with him recently and he said: "What do you think of all the warming up the players do now? Our warm-up was jumping up and down a bit in the changing room and then walking up the steps and on to the pitch." I watched him play in some very exciting games.

Ken Kelly was still the captain and I remember we went on strike in the changing room before one match as we were getting changed. The board had changed our bonuses for the Challenge Cup and the Lancashire Cup. We had a set fee until we got to the quarter-finals and then we had a bonus, with bigger bonuses for the semi-final and final. We drew a struggling Second Division team at home in the quarter-finals and it was one of those games we were going to win even if we had put the 'A' team out. We were on something ridiculous like £750 a man. The crowd wouldn't have covered the wage bill and so the board decided they were going to drop the bonus back down to £250. Ken said: "No, we are going on strike." The board then offered us £550. Ken asked us if we were all right with that. I was all right with £250 to be honest because I was still a young lad.

Another time, it was a bitterly cold and freezing winter's night, like it used to be, and Ken Kelly and Dave Chisnall were convinced the game was going to be called off. Anyway, the referee said it was fit enough to play. Ken and Chissie and lot of the older heads said: "No. The ground is definitely too hard sir." We always had respect for referees, not like in football, where players go up and bark in the referees' faces. It was always "Yes sir and no sir", but the referee wouldn't change his mind. "Right," said Ken. "If we are playing, we will have to have a drink before we go out." Ken disappeared into the directors' lounge and came back with a bottle of sherry and made us all have a drink. I felt really sick and I thought "This isn't going to help me play, never mind keep me warm" but they were the old ways and we had to do it because Ken said and Chissie said and we didn't disrespect them because of their experience and wealth of knowledge.

Kevin Ashcroft was another very loud coach and whatever he wanted to call you or tell you it would echo around Wilderspool or around the dressing room. One Christmas Eve, before the Warrington versus Widnes match on Boxing Day, we were all messing about in training because it was Christmas and Kevin said: "I'll tell you what. I want you all in tomorrow morning." We said: "You're having a laugh. It's Christmas Day." But he wasn't joking and so we all had to train on Christmas morning. It wasn't too bad for me because I only lived in Howley, but the Yorkshire lads and the Cumbrian lads weren't very happy. They had all wanted to go home after we finished training on Christmas Eve. But Kevin had us all in on Christmas morning.

Kevin signed Mick Blacker from Halifax. He was an outstanding half-back, even though he was coming to the end of his career. He had great hands – and he could look after himself. They used to call it Mick Blacker's "blackout elbow" because he used it like a rabbit punch and flattened people.

In the 1982–83 season, when I scored my first try for Warrington, Bob Eccles scored 37 tries in 37 matches: a club record for a forward. Bob was a fast forward before his time.

Left: Mark scored his first four-point try for Warrington at Blackpool in September 1983. He picked up a loose ball near halfway and sprinted 40 yards to the corner, going outside two defenders. He had already scored a three-point try away to Hull KR the previous season.

Bottom: Mark scored his first try at Wilderspool, against Hull KR in September 1983. He went on to score another 100 tries on the famous old ground.
(Both photos: Eddie Fuller)

He was lucky enough to have a great half-back playing with him in Ken Kelly. Ken found him and he had speed to burn when most forwards were shaped like ale barrels. When I went to play for Brisbane Norths, we shared an apartment. Also that season, Phil Ford scored 20 tries. He was a one-off. He was elusive and either had an excellent game or a poor game, like a few wingers who have followed, the likes of Richard Henare. He was the same, either fantastic or pretty ordinary.

At the start of the 1983–84 season, we got our first shirt sponsors, Sparkomatic, who made car stereos and were based in Crewe. Some of the lads went down to Earls Court for the Motor Show for a week, but I was struggling with an injury and had to stay behind. I don't know how you model a car stereo, but they did. Later on we also did some photo shoots with Tracey Elvik, the page three girl from Warrington, which was nice. We also did some modelling for *The Clothes Show* with Jeff Banks. We had to dress up as YMCA characters with moustaches, leather trousers and leather belts in a freezing cold aircraft hangar at Burtonwood Air Base. They made us look fools really, but they said "whatever you do, don't steal any of the gear" because the false moustaches were worth £500 each and the leather belts cost £150 each just because they had Jeff Banks' name on them.

St Helens 26 Warrington 30
Wednesday, 14 September 1983, Lancashire Cup second round
This was only my fourth game for the first team and I only remember a bit of it because I was one of five players sent off. It wasn't going particularly well and it was one of those nasty games which Warrington versus St Helens always was at the time. They were always full on, blood and guts and glory, no mic-ed up referees, no cameras, no video refs, no referees in the stands and the players could get away with a little bit more. There were late tackles going in, feet going in, fists and forearms. It got a bit tasty and I ended up fighting with one of the hardest lads in rugby league at the time: Roy Haggerty. I stood my ground. He closed my eyes with punches, I closed his, we were both sent off and we have been mates ever since. I was banned for six matches for that and so was Roy. Phil Ford and Mal Yates of Warrington and Steve Peters, from St Helens, were also sent off by Stan Wall.

Roy Haggerty was a lovely bloke; off the pitch. He went on the Great Britain tour of Australia in 1988 and there is a funny story that he was the first off the plane at Brisbane Airport and the customs officer asked him where he was from and Roy said: "The top of Elephant Lane." Very helpful. Four days after the St Helens match we played Hull KR at home and I scored my first try at Wilderspool. Little did I know then that it would be the first of 101 I would score on the famous old ground.

The suspension ruled me out for all of October and I made my comeback for the 'A' team in a friendly against Lancashire Amateurs at Wilderspool on a Wednesday night in November. Dave Chisnall played prop and I proved my fitness by scoring a hat-trick of tries in the first half as centre to Phil Ford. It was my first hat-trick in the primrose and blue of Warrington.

In November, Kevin Ashcroft signed Pat Poasa, a Maori prop from the West End club in New Zealand. He was an absolute giant and ended up marrying a Warrington girl. The club had to have special shorts made for him. We all wore 32 inches, 34 inches or 36 inches. He had 52 inches. He had the biggest legs I have ever seen. When Pat was playing we hated being on the bench because the subs had to rub him down. There were no masseurs in those days. We would try and sneak out of the dressing room, but Kevin Ashcroft would say: "Make sure his legs are warm."

When Pat arrived, he wanted to taste a local drink and so we sent him into the bar and told him to ask for a Split Dick. We told him it was Guinness with Black in it. He asked the girl behind the bar and she told him he would have a Split Lip if he was cheeky to her again like that. She asked him who had told him to ask for that and then she saw a gang of players behind him and knew it was us.

John Bevan was my centre then and I used to tell people that was because I was faster than John which probably wasn't true. I remember a game at Wilderspool when fans used to sit in front of the Wilderspool Centre. It was another bitterly cold day and John must have been feeling it and went into the stand and asked one fan if he could have a drink of his soup and borrow his gloves. The fan said "Yes" and John came back on the field wearing gloves and asked the referee if it was OK. The referee said "No" and so John had to give them back.

One day when we were training at Victoria Park, John arrived and put his work boots on. We thought he had left his trainers at home by mistake, but he said he had not. He said he trained as hard and fast as he could in his work boots so that when he put his proper boots on for a match they felt much lighter. John was as fit as a fiddle. His wife, Rhiannon, used to take us for what would now be called boot camp training or aerobics. This was in the early 1980s.

Ronnie Duane had a great season in 1983–84 and was picked by Frank Myler for the Great Britain tour of Australia and New Zealand that summer. We had played together at Woolston Rovers and he was to be the number one Great Britain centre on the tour, ahead of Ellery Hanley and Garry Schofield. However, he tore knee ligaments after only eight minutes of the opening match against Northern Territory in Darwin. Hanley and Schofield became the centre partnership after that and Ronnie's never been the same since. He had his knee operated on in Australia and is still suffering with it. These days they would ice up the knee, send the player back home and have the best surgeons in the world look at him.

Closer to home, we were winning a trophy: the Seven Seas Sevens tournament at Hull in May 1984. We took a young, fast and mobile side: Phil Ford, Mike Gregory, John Fieldhouse, Paul Cullen, Brian Carbert, Billy McGinty, Ken Kelly (captain), Paul Fellows and me. We beat Bradford Northern and Oldham and then Hull in the final and our prize was as many vitamin tablets as we wanted – courtesy of the sponsors.

There were a lot of changes that summer: Peter Higham replaced Brian Pitchford as Warrington chairman and Reg Bowden, the former Widnes and Fulham scrum-half, was appointed player-coach.

Left: Mark having a dislocated shoulder popped back in its joint by the Warrington physio during a break in play.

Right: Mark joins John Bevan after Bevan had scored a try against Huddersfield in the Challenge Cup at Wilderspool, February 1984.

Left: Mark touches down in the corner at Leigh on Easter Monday 1984. A supporter has her camera at the ready.

(All photos: Eddie Fuller)

Above: Three Oldham players try to catch Mark.

Left: Mark scored Warrington's first try in a 19–16 win at Bradford in April 1984.

(Both photos: Eddie Fuller)

I got on very well with Peter. He was a Warrington lad like me and we are still friends. I still pop into the Vice Presidents Lounge at the Halliwell Jones Stadium on match days to see him. Contract talks with Peter were quite straightforward. If the player wanted £50, they asked for £75, Peter offered £25 and they met in the middle.

Reg had been Fulham's player-coach for the previous four years and brought Bob Jackson to Wilderspool with him. Bob was one of the first Australian forwards to come over after the transfer ban was lifted. Bob hit the ground running and was a great success. Reg returned to Fulham and signed Steve Diamond, Hussein M'Barki and Dave Allen. They all struggled with injuries and form, but Bob was brilliant. He was an 80-minute forward and very mobile. He was great to have in the starting line-up.

Reg also signed Paul Younane from Parramatta. He was a skilful centre or half-back with a side-step and was a quiet Australian. I will say that again in case you missed it the first time. He was a quiet Australian. He kept himself to himself, did his job, trained well and was a model professional.

Reg took an instant liking to me and gave me a proper chance in the first team. He also gave Paul Bishop his debut at scrum-half at the age of 17 – against Workington Town at Wilderspool in October 1984. Paul scored a try and kicked seven goals as we won 42–30. His second full appearance came against Oldham at Wilderspool the following month and I will never forget it because Paul swallowed his tongue. I was on the left wing and we were playing towards the Railway End. Green Vigo, the South African Oldham winger, who was an absolute gentleman of the game, caught Paul with a hard, but fair, tackle. It was just an ordinary tackle, nothing dirty about it, nothing malicious, but Paul swallowed his tongue and started having convulsions. It was 10 yards from the Oldham dugout where Paul's brother, Gary, who was an Oldham player, was sitting. He saw it all. Dr Rothwell, the Warrington club doctor, rushed on with a Biro and a safety pin. He hooked Paul's tongue out of his throat with the Biro and pinned it to his bottom lip to save his life.

I played with Gary for Brisbane Norths in Australia the following summer and we talked about the incident. He said it was the longest few minutes of his life. Before it happened Green Vigo had been his best mate at the club, but afterwards he didn't even like to talk to him because it brought the memories flooding back.

Every Thursday night after Warrington training, 10 of us used to go to the Carlton nightclub. Reg tried to ban us. One Thursday night the doorman ran up the stairs and said: "Reg is coming up." So we all scattered and hid under tables and in the toilets. Reg walked in and he had a sheepskin bomber jacket on. He stuck out like a sore thumb. It was like something out of the *Pink Panther* films with players hiding behind curtains with their feet showing. Reg made the DJ stop the music, turn all the lights on and tried to find us. He found about half of us. At training on the Saturday morning he absolutely flogged us and we ended up pulling off a shock win the following day. Going to the Carlton club on a Thursday was a tradition but I am not sure the lads would get away with it now under Tony Smith.

Barrow 7 Warrington 14

Sunday 16 December 1984, Slalom Lager Championship

Reg picked me as a stand-off for this game and we won so I couldn't have done too badly, but I never played at number six again. For the next match, at Leigh on Boxing Day, there was another unusual stand-off – John Bevan – and we won that match too. Most of my appearances for Warrington though were on the wing and I was happy to play on either side. A lot depended on who my centre was. A lot of centres stepped off their inside foot and went over to their winger. In later years Toa Kohe-Love played on the wrong side for about five seasons at Warrington until he was swapped over. He was always going off his outside foot and going back into play away from his winger.

Warrington 48 Hunslet 16

Sunday 6 January 1985, Slalom Lager Championship

John Bevan scored his 200th try for Warrington in this match while I was a non-playing substitute again. Non-playing substitutes are not very common now, even though there are four subs instead of the two when I was playing. It is a 17-man game now. Later that month we signed Andy Gregory, the Great Britain scrum-half, from Widnes in a world record deal. He was the on-field general we needed and a massive signing for us.

Saturday 2 February, 1985

I went shopping in Warrington town centre and sometime between 1.30pm and 4.30pm I lost the silver identity bracelet I was wearing. The bracelet had my name engraved on it. John Dickens, the sports editor at the *Warrington Guardian*, put an appeal in the paper for me, asking if anyone finding it could return it to the club. Sadly, no one did, but – even though it is now 30 years later – there's still time.

Andy Gregory published his autobiography, *Pint Size*, in 2000 and in it, starting on page 53, there is a story about a night out that Andy and his first wife, Dawn, and me and my then girlfriend, Gaynor, had in Warrington in February 1985. Sad to say it ended up in a massive fight with the Cross Keys pub football team. There were 17 of them and two of us. It got out of hand. The landlord threw the football team out and let us finish our drinks. Then he asked us to leave, which had given the football team enough time to form a semi-circle around the door, waiting for us. They kicked us all the way down to the Hop Pole, which is probably 100 to 150 yards. So we were fighting up-and-down the High Street.

At the time, the actor Don Johnson, in the television series *Miami Vice*, had started carrying his money in his shirt pocket and I was doing the same. Well, my shirt got ripped off in the fight before Andy Greg and myself were arrested. The police released us fairly quickly and we went for something to eat at the Hoi Tin Chinese restaurant and it was only then that I realised that all my money was gone. We walked back across town and I found my shirt in the gutter, three hours after the fight, with all my money still in the pocket. Dozens of people must have walked past it and not realised.

Warrington's 1984–85 squad. Left to right, back: Roy Campbell, Mark Gleave, Paul Fellows, Bob Eccles, Phil Ford, Tony Worrall, Steve Moylan, Mark Forster. Second row: Tony Barrow ('A' team coach), Steve Morris, Brian Carbert, Carl Webb, Mike Gregory, Bob Jackson, Mark Roberts, Barry Peters, Tommy Gittens, Reg Bowden (coach). Third row: physio, Alan Scott, John Fieldhouse, Billy McGinty, Paul Ford, Roger O'Mahony. Front: Paul Bishop, Billy Cowell, Tommy Rawlinson, Peter Halpin, Paul Cullen, John Kerr, Ken Kelly.

Mark looking for a gap between Kevin Tamati (right) and one of the O'Neill brothers against Widnes at Wilderspool, September 1984.

(Both photos: Eddie Fuller)

24

Mark about to score a try at Leigh, September 1984.

Beating New Zealander Gary Kemble to score a try against Hull at Wilderspool in September 1984. Cliff Hodgson from Maryport is the referee.

Mark scored two tries, but then broke a bone in his left hand while making a tackle in the last minute.

(Both photos: Eddie Fuller)

Dawn was worried about the trouble and asked the police if she would end up with a police record. The officer saw the funny side of it and said he had *Walking on the Moon*. He said she been watching too many episodes of *The Bill*.

At the police station, the Chief Superintendent had taken Andy and myself into his office and told us that we were not to blame, but obviously we had been in a fight, which was a serious matter. He put us on bail and told us not to leave the country. I put my hand up like a 12-year-old schoolboy and said that I had a contract to go to Australia for three months that summer. "Oh," he said. "If we have to call you back, will you come back?" "Of course," I said, with my fingers crossed. I wasn't going to say "No" was I? So I went to Australia for three months and left Andy to sort out all the mither and deal with the press.

As I said earlier, I am always late, but at the end of March 1985, Warrington hooker Steve Moylan, who had played alongside me in the 'A' team, did something that I have never done – he missed a kick-off. It was the weekend when the clocks went forward one hour to signal the start of British Summer Time and Steve forgot. We all arrived, except Steve, and this was before mobile phones, so he could not be contacted, and Carl Webb, who was 16th man, came in for him. The first we saw of Steve was at half-time. He said he had been driving to the ground with the window open because it was a hot day and he could hear the roar of the crowd. He thought to himself "there must be some amazing pre-match entertainment today, the crowd's going mad". It was only when he parked at the ground and got out of his car that he realised he had missed the kick-off. Steve never lived it down. For the next two or three years, when the clocks went forward, people would ring him up and remind him. Steve never started a first team game for Warrington again and joined Salford in November 1985 after their hooker Paul Groves broke his leg.

4. Brisbane Norths

In the summer of 1985, Bob Eccles and I went to play for Brisbane Norths. Warrington were supposed to send their best forward and their best back. Ken Kelly was the captain and the best back, but his wife wouldn't let him go and so I went instead. I said I didn't mind being second best if I got to go to Australia. It wasn't a massive contract, but it was all part of the learning curve. Two players from Oldham, back Gary Bishop and forward Mick Worrall, joined the same club.

After my first match, we all went out for a meal in the restaurant next door and a chance to meet the guys, players like Trevor 'The Axe' Gillmeister, the Walters brothers – Kerrod, Kevin and Steve – and an enormous prop called Zulu. They told me that because we were players we didn't have to pay. We just walked out when we'd finished. I thought to myself: "I'm going to like this Brisbane lark." So when the bill came I walked out and as we went through the door they shouted: "Run!" We ran around the building as fast as we could and back to the clubhouse. I was one of the first back and who was waiting, but the three chefs from the restaurant, saying: "Pay your bill sir." I couldn't believe it and tried to explain about being a player and being told I didn't have to pay. By now the rest of the team were there and just started laughing. It was my initiation to Brisbane rugby league. The chefs were in on it, the players were in on it and the staff were in on it. Everyone except me.

I was there for three months and enjoyed every minute of it. It was a long way from home for a young lad, I was only 20, but it was great fun. Four of us shared a Datsun and we used to put two dollars of petrol in at a time. When the petrol ran out we would just leave the car where it was until the next person needed it. "Is there any petrol in it?" "No, but the can's in the boot."

Bob Eccles and I went over first. We were staying in a two-bedroom apartment, a typical rugby player's apartment, and my fiancée Gaynor followed later. There was a massive picture – about six feet by five feet – of a naked woman on the wall and Gaynor's first words were: "That's coming down straight away." And it did.

In June I went to Lang Park – which is now known as the Suncorp Stadium – to see the first Test between Australia and New Zealand. The match is still famous today because of a huge fight between Kevin Tamati and Greg Dowling. They started fighting in the middle of the pitch and were both sin-binned by the French referee, Julien Rascagneres. Then they had a fight halfway off the pitch and were separated again. Then they had a third fight when they reached the barriers. In an interview 23 years later with *The Sydney Daily Telegraph*, Tamati revealed that Dowling had subjected him to racist abuse, calling him a "nigger" and a "black bastard". Kevin said he did not think that Dowling was a racist. He had just said things he should not have said in the heat of battle. No wonder Kevin was angry.

Locker Cup winners 1985: Left to right, back: Bob Jackson, Carl Webb, Glyn Shaw, Paul Cullen, Brian Carbert, Mark Forster, Mark Roberts, Paul Ford, Ronnie Duane; front: Andy Gregory, Tony Worrall, Ken Kelly (captain), Bob Eccles, Mike Gregory. (Photo: Eddie Whitham)

I made some great friends in Brisbane and met Kevin Walters again when he came to play for Warrington in 2001. He rang his brother Steve and said: "You'll never guess who I am having a pint with." Steve said: "I don't give a damn. It's four o'clock in the morning here."

It was tough playing back-to-back seasons – 1984–85 in England, 1985 in Australia and 1985–86 in England – but I wasn't really fond of pre-season training and it got me out of that. A lot of people have said that if I had done more pre-season training and had a better diet – I don't like fruit and salad – I could have played for longer. I say: "I played for 21 years. How long do you want me to play for?" Even now my grandchildren Taylor and Maisie will stuff a banana or an orange in my face because they have been told by their mum and their gran that I don't particularly like fruit. Then they shuffle away giggling.

When I got back from Australia in July 1985, I discovered that Warrington had signed Kevin Tamati from Widnes, Les Boyd from Manly and Alan Rathbone from Bradford Northern: three hard forwards. Peter Higham, the Warrington chairman, joked that he had had to sign all three because it was very unlikely that they would all play together. One or more would always be suspended. I remember going to Featherstone and on the coach there we watched a *Rocky* film. But that wasn't such a great idea with Les Boyd, Kevin Tamati and Bob Jackson in the front row. There were three mass brawls in the first 20 minutes and two of them spent time in the sin bin. We never watched any *Rocky* films on the way to games after that. The facilities at Post Office Road in those days were pretty

28

basic too. After we were strapped up and rubbed down in the changing room we had to go outside to use the public toilet with the supporters. So we would be peeing up against the wall with Featherstone and Warrington fans on either side.

Warrington had also signed centre Phil Blake from Manly, a young kid we had never heard of. But he scored 22 tries in 19 appearances the following season and made a name for himself. He was a genius with the ball, his footwork was unbelievable and he was fast, although we thought he didn't like tackling. He was one of the original male models, an early David Beckham or Josh Charnley. He liked his hair, scar-less face and full set of teeth, so he wasn't into hard graft. He was just happy to score tries in a side that could look after him, with Les Boyd, Kevin Tamati, Bob Jackson, Mark Roberts, Billy McGinty, Mike Gregory and Alan Rathbone. With that lot in the side Phil didn't have to make many tackles.

Les Boyd made his debut in the Lancashire Cup semi-final against Widnes at Wilderspool and we won 11–4 to reach the final. I was still only 20 and it was my first final. It was against Wigan at Knowsley Road in front of a 19,202 crowd. It doesn't get much better than that. I started on the bench but came on when Phil Blake was injured in the first half. It was an amazing match. Another of our new signings, Australian full-back Brian Johnson, raced in for a try from 80 yards and Brian Carbert kicked two goals to put us 8–2 ahead. But Wigan, including new signing Ellery Hanley, hit back with five tries to win 34–8. Alan Rathbone was sent off for a late tackle on Ian Potter and later banned for six matches. Andy Gregory was also sent off, for allegedly stamping on South African forward Nick Du Toit, although he was later found not guilty.

Warrington 34 Barrow 14
Sunday 1 December 1985, John Player Special Trophy
My 21st birthday was on 25 November and I celebrated in style with four tries in my next match, this one. It was one of those games when everything went right for me. Paul Cullen was my centre that day and he wasn't renowned for making tries for his winger, but he did that afternoon. I was the man-of-the-match and so I got a trophy and I think a £25 bonus from the sponsor. But we lost at home to Wigan in the next round and again in the league on New Year's Day and the pressure was starting to mount on Reg Bowden.

Warrington wanted instant success and Reg was still seen as a player-coach rather than a coach in his own right. He always had the respect of the players, but just wasn't getting the results on the field. Finally, after we lost 13–6 at Oldham in the Challenge Cup in March, Reg was told that his contract would not be renewed at the end of the season and so he resigned. He had only been in charge for 20 months. Reg's assistant, Tony Barrow, became caretaker coach until the end of the season. When we first got a gym at Wilderspool, Tony said he wanted us all there every night after work. I said to Tony that the only way he would get me in the gym was if he put a bar in the corner. He chased me around the dressing room, kicking me up the backside and made me go to the gym every night for a fortnight. With Tony in charge I knew it was going to be hard work, but that it was going to be worth it.

Four tries against Barrow at Wilderspool, December 1985

Left: On an 80-yard run to the line.

Below: About to touch down.

(Both photos: Eddie Fuller)

Just the full-back to beat. (Both photos: Eddie Fuller)

The 1985 Lancashire Cup Final

Being introduced with Phil Blake (4) and Mike Gregory (12) before the match against Wigan at Knowsley Road. Coach Reg Bowden is in the background.

Action from the match. (Both photos: Eddie Whitham)

On one occasion we stopped at a service station on the way back from a match and I was talking to my mum and dad about the game. They went to every match. When I looked around the team coach had gone. Mum and dad gave me a lift back to Wilderspool and we actually beat the coach back, but Tony Barrow still gave me a bollocking for missing the bus. It was Tony's way of letting me know that he was in charge.

On another occasion, in April 1986, we played at York in the league and, after the match, I got talking to one of the York lads who was in the Great Britain under–21s squad with me. Once again I missed the coach but, luckily enough, there was a supporters' coach waiting to leave and I got a lift back with them. They were made up because we had won 34–6. Again we beat the team coach back, but again Tony wiped the floor with me.

If Tony said something we knew he meant it. If he told us to do something we did it and we knew he would never go behind our backs. We were his protégés because he had signed us for the 'A' team. He let us enjoy our game and our social life because we were still only part-time and a lot of us used to work for him as well. He was in the construction industry. He used to say that he employed us so that he could keep an eye on us. He also let us be our own rugby player. He used to say: "Why would I sign you as a stand-off and then play you on the wing or at loose-forward or hooker?" His team talks before the game and at half-time always contained lots of "f's and b's" and other obscenities, but he always finished it with: if it kicks off, one in, all in, the referee can't send you all off.

Tony gave Gary Sanderson his debut in the second row. Gary was from Thatto Heath in St Helens, like Tony, and was a very under-rated player. He would tackle like mad and also drive the ball in at least once in every set of six. He was a great servant to the club. He earned the nickname 'The Hoover' because of his low tackling technique. He would hit players between the knees and ankles and bring them down. How he didn't get injured I don't know.

Under Tony we won our last six league games of the season to finish fourth in the table. Our reward was a home tie against Widnes in the first round of the Premiership Trophy and, with two minutes left, we were losing 8–6. Then Paul Bishop made a break, sprinted clear and sent Ronnie Duane in for the match-winning try. A trip to Wigan in the semi-finals was up next and again it was the Paul Bishop show. He kicked a record-breaking five drop goals – and scored a try – as we won 23–12.

Warrington 38 Halifax 10
Sunday 18 May 1986, Premiership Final, Elland Road
The pinnacle of Tony Barrow's coaching career at Warrington was winning the 1986 Premiership final. We had a great team including Les Boyd, Brian Johnson, Andy Gregory, Mark Roberts and Mike Gregory. It was a fantastic day and I was lucky enough to get on the scoresheet. Les Boyd won the Harry Sunderland Trophy as man-of-the-match and Tony was confirmed as Warrington coach by Peter Higham during the celebrations in the changing room.

It was strange playing with Les Boyd. It was like he had a dual character, two people. Off the field, he was as nice as pie, but as soon as he walked over the touchline it was like somebody else possessed his body and he was just an animal. He had an aura about him. He was the great Les Boyd and every English, Australian or New Zealand prop wanted to fill him in. I remember once we were playing Wigan at Wilderspool and Henderson Gill gave Boydy a bit of a slap, a cheap dig. Les wasn't happy. He played the ball and decided to chase Henderson around the pitch. He was never going to catch him but it was funny to watch. It was just like it was a schoolboys under–10s game. Henderson was running round players just to keep away from Les. Off the field Les was a gentleman. He was one of the best players to come over from Australia and on one of the best contracts because he was the great Les Boyd. After a match at Wilderspool he used to come into the players' bar where there was a pool table that was always covered up. He used to sit on the pool table with a pint of orange squash with one of his kids, Grant, under one arm and Alisha, under the other arm. Three of them sharing a pint of orange squash and he was on one of the best contracts.

Left: Mark chasing the ball against Hull KR in 1984–85. (Photo: Eddie Fuller)

Below: Mark scoring against Dewsbury, April 1986 (Photo Eddie Whitham)

The 1986 Premiership Final against Halifax at Elland Road.

Left: Mark racing in for a try.
(Photo: Eddie Fuller)

Middle: Running around the pitch after winning the Premiership Trophy in May 1986. Mark Forster (left), with Paul Cullen (centre) and Mark Roberts.
(Photo: Eddie Fuller)

Bottom: Captain Les Boyd with the Premiership Trophy. Left to right: Brian Carbert, Billy McGinty, Paul Bishop, Paul Ford, Paul Cullen, Ronnie Duane, Mark Forster, Gary Sanderson, Mike Gregory.
(Photo: Eddie Whitham)

5. Fastest man in rugby league

In February 1985 Maurice Bamford, the Great Britain manager, had added me to his Great Britain Under–21s training squad. By June, there were four Warrington players in the squad: Billy McGinty, Brian Carbert, Barry Peters and me. Brian and I made our debuts against the touring New Zealand side at Bradford that October – but only just.

As usual, there was a pile-up on the M62 and a huge traffic jam. So we drove along the hard shoulder. Inevitably, we were stopped by the police. We told them what was happening and they checked our story. Then they told us that the kick-off had been delayed because of the accident and so we could get back on the motorway and leave the hard shoulder clear.

New Zealand put out a strong side with Joe Ropati, who later joined Warrington, in the centre, Shane Cooper, who later joined St Helens, at stand-off and prop Kurt Sorensen, who was soon to sign for Widnes, on the bench.

We lost 16–12, but produced a good performance. Hull loose-forward Gary Divorty was our man-of-the-match and created tries for me and Shaun Edwards. I played in the centre, with Brian on the wing and Brian kicked two goals. I would play anywhere for Great Britain, except the front row of course.

Three months later, we travelled to St Esteve in France to play the French Espoirs, their under–24 side. Shaun Wane, then a young Wigan prop and now Wigan coach, was our captain. Even then we could tell he was a leader. He was already a regular in the Wigan team. He crashed over for a try in the first half, but we still lost 19–6. He has taken his passion for the game into his coaching.

Two weeks later, in February 1986, we got our own back with a 6–2 win on a freezing night in Whitehaven. Brian Carbert scored all of our points with a try and a penalty goal. Roy Powell, the Leeds prop or second row, played in all three games. He loved the gym. He was going to the gym more times than we trained. We all turned up as fast, skinny kids, but he was an absolute monster. It was clear that he was going to be a successful pro.

He went on to play for Bradford Northern, Featherstone Rovers and Batley and win 19 Great Britain caps and go on tour in 1988. I could not believe it when he collapsed and died, aged just 33, before a training session with his new club Rochdale Hornets in December 1998.

Maurice Bamford was a very good coach and motivator. He was a bit like Alex Murphy in that he liked to get his teams fired up before a match. I remember going into camp at the National Sports Centre at Lilleshall with him before a Great Britain game. He said on the night before the game he wanted us to do what we normally did. If we normally went to bed at 7pm then go to bed at 7pm. If we normally went to bed at 11pm then go to bed at 11pm. If we normally had two pints then have two pints. But if your room-mate normally has two pints and you don't then, you don't have to. His man-management was fantastic.

Warrington won 28–6 in the 1986 Locker Cup match against Wigan at Central Park with Mark scoring two tries. Kevin Meadows is the Warrington number 14. (Both photos: Eddie Fuller)

I made my debut for Lancashire against Yorkshire in the War of the Roses match at Headingley in September 1986. Alex Murphy, who was the St Helens coach at the time, was the Lancashire coach as well. We were late setting off for the match because he had bet on a horse and wanted to know the result before we left Knowsley Road. It was a Wednesday night match and we were waiting for the result of the 4pm race at Haydock Park before we set off. On the coach, Andy Gregory asked him how his horse got on and Murphy said: "It got beat and you bastards best not get beat tonight." We got stuck in the tea-time traffic around Leeds and were a bit late arriving.

Yorkshire had Ellery Hanley and Henderson Gill in their team. They both scored tries as Yorkshire won 26–14. The following morning I drove to work from Orford to Lymm and asked the site engineer what I was doing that day. I opened the back of my van and discovered that all my tools had been stolen. The thieves must have known I was playing for Lancashire, the match might even have been on television, and they robbed me while I was on the pitch.

I played for Lancashire again three years later when Doug Laughton was the coach. This time the match was at Central Park, but it didn't make any difference. We were 32–0 down at half-time and lost 56–12, but at least I didn't have my tools stolen that time.

I still think there is a place for a Lancashire versus Yorkshire series today. It is a stepping stone to the international scene. Some players are fantastic at club level, but when they take the next step – the next two steps really – to international level it is too much for them. They either freeze, panic or are out of their depth. Lancashire versus Yorkshire should be like the State of Origin series in Australia which they use to pick their national side. The Kangaroos aren't the 17 best club players, they are the 17 best State of Origin players.

The chief executives of the Super League clubs wouldn't like a return of Lancashire versus Yorkshire because it would be two more matches for the top players, the crowd pleasers. But if we are ever going to catch up to Australia and New Zealand then I think we need to bring Lancashire versus Yorkshire back.

Throughout my career I was called many names and many things: "the oldest winger in town", "the Peter Pan of rugby league" and, of course, "the fastest man in rugby league" after winning the title in November 1986. The rules were simple enough. Wearing a rugby kit and boots and carrying a ball, we had to run from one goal line to the other and touch down to stop the clock.

My heat was before the first test between Great Britain and Australia at Old Trafford. I was up against Barrie Ledger (St Helens), Les Quirk (Barrow), John Henderson (Leigh) and New Zealander Mark Bournville (Swinton). I won the heat – and I was easing up towards the end – and Barrie was second; so we both went through to the final.

The second heat was before the second test match at Elland Road and two Australians – Andrew Ettingshausen (Leeds) and Kerry Boustead (Hull KR) – went through. They beat David Plange (Castleford), Courtney Thompson (Mansfield) and David Laws (Hull KR).

The fastest man in rugby league

Left: Mark was presented with a silver salver and £250 after winning a sprint challenge at Headingley in August 1986. (Photo: Eddie Fuller)

Middle: The race to find the fastest man in rugby league. From the left are Kerry Boustead (Hull KR), Barrie Ledger (St Helens), Andrew Ettingshausen (Leeds) and Mark Forster (Warrington).
(Photo: Eddie Whitham)

Bottom: Mark with the silver salver and cheque for £1,000 with beaten rivals Barrie Ledger (left), Andrew Ettingshausen (centre) and Kerry Boustead.
(Photo: Eddie Whitham)

40

The final was before the third test at Central Park and we were all on the start line, wearing Whitbread Trophy Bitter shirts after the sponsors. For some reason, and I don't know why, possibly some sort of psychology, just before the referee was about to blow his whistle to start the race, I dropped the ball and kicked it for about five or 10 yards. The other lads said "What are you doing?" and lost their concentration. I said: "I dropped the ball, I'm sorry." But all the time I was still focused and when the race actually started I won it easily. I got a cheque for £1,000 and a silver salver. My then girlfriend and now wife Gaynor was sitting in the stand with an Argos catalogue out, wondering what she could spend the prize on. I always blame her dad, Colin Jordan, for me and Gaynor getting together. He was the steward at the Touchdown Club at Wilderspool and the players always used to go in there after games and training. Gaynor, who was a legal secretary with the Warrington solicitors Ridgway Sephton, and I got to know each other. Then we started going out properly after a night out at the Carlton club.

Warrington thought it would be a good idea to generate some publicity out of me being the fastest man in rugby league and for me to check how fast I could run against a police radar on Wilderspool Causeway. I didn't think it was such a good idea because I had just been fined for speeding myself and the copper had said to me: "You are not only fast on the field, you are fast in the car, aren't you Mark?" I had about 19 goes at it over two days, but the police radar couldn't pinpoint me and so we had to give up. So we never actually found out how fast I could run. With the technology today it could easily be done. And I still had to pay my speeding fine. My best time for the 100 metres, when I was at my fastest, was about 11 and a half seconds and that was carrying a ball and in rugby boots. So that was pretty fast.

Dennis Hunt, who was Warrington's sprint coach for about 13 years from 1976 to 1989, had a personal best time of 10.7 seconds for the 100 metres. He told me that only two Warrington players ever beat him in a race – me and Ken Kelly. I beat him because I was faster. Ken beat him because he tripped Dennis up.

Four years after I became the fastest man in rugby league, around 1990, the RFL rang and asked me to defend my title but I had been out for two weeks with a hamstring injury. I said the club would go mad if I entered, but they said they had spoken to Warrington and they had given their approval. I then spoke to Peter Higham, the Warrington chairman, and Brian Johnson, the Warrington coach, and they said I could enter as long as I didn't go flat out. I said: "OK, not a problem." Martin Offiah won it and got something like £750 and I got £500 for appearing and jogging behind him. I didn't go flat out – the video shows that – and he only beat me by two metres. So maybe, if I had been fully fit, with no hamstring problems and allowed to go flat out, I would have beaten him.

A lot of people say Martin Offiah was the best winger at the time, but he was just quick. If he wasn't shown the outside a defence could cope with Martin. I was lucky enough to turn and catch him twice – once when he was at Widnes and once when he was at Wigan. The winger I didn't like playing against was Jason Robinson – small, nippy and he could duck under me if I went for a big hit.

41

Left: Mark zooms down the wing, past groundsman Roy 'Ockher' Aspinall and the club doctor, Dr Rothwell, in the tunnel during the 1986–87 season.

Below: Mark scores against Widnes in the John Player Special Trophy semi–final at Central Park in December 1986. Steve O'Neill is the Widnes prop.

(Both photos: Eddie Fuller)

John Player Special Trophy Final

Mark (number 5) introduced to the Mayor of Bolton by Les Boyd before the final against Wigan at Burnden Park in January 1987. Ken Kelly is next in line.

Mark beat Ellery Hanley to score in front of 21,000 fans. (Both photos: Eddie Fuller)

A defender couldn't take his eyes off him for a second and if he did he would be round them and gone. The defender would be left grasping at air. That's why they called him 'Billy Whizz'. Andrew Ettingshausen, of Leeds, was as fast as anyone and he had a side-step. Eric Grothe, in his Leeds days, was enormous. He was bigger than Les Boyd and Steve Roach and could shift as well. The thought of tackling him gave me nightmares for two days before. I did all right actually. I just stood in front of him for the whole match and didn't let the ball get to him. In the end he said: "Will you get out of my face?" But I always respected every player who pulls a shirt on.

Joe Ropati joined Warrington in October 1986 and scored 19 tries during the 1986–87 season. He was a beast of a man – and a character. One day I borrowed his club car – I think it was a Maestro or something like that – and was driving through Stockton Heath when Joe jumped on the bonnet and dented it. He virtually wrote the car off, he was that big. Later on, he took the car back to Wilderspool and they asked him: "What's happened to the car?" Joe said: "I don't know. It was like that when I got up this morning."

Warrington 24 Barrow 20
Monday 19 January 1987, Stones Bitter Championship
Believe it or not, this match was played at Maine Road, Manchester City's ground. Wilderspool was frozen solid and so the club switched the game to Maine Road to prevent a fixture backlog building up. Sadly, only 2,000 fans turned up. Tony Thorniley, another player from Woolston Rovers, my old club, made his debut as a substitute, aged 20. Tony developed into a top-class centre, but he suffered a neck injury and the treatment at the time was to put him on a stretching machine like a medieval rack. His neck was stretched and any displaced discs would fall back in place naturally. After two or three months of this treatment every other day, he came back for pre-season training and was two inches taller. To this day we still call him 'Too Tall'.

In 1987 rugby league became one of the first sports to introduce drug testing and I suppose I must have been one of the first players to be tested. In those days a player could only be tested on a match day. When the testers arrived two players per team had their numbers drawn out of a bag and, at the end of the game, the testers would be waiting in the tunnel. They were not allowed to leave your side until you had provided a sample. They would follow you into the toilet cubicle. They gave you as much water as you wanted, but you could only drink water they supplied in specially sealed cartons. Normally, after a game, you wanted to go to the toilet, but as soon as the tester asked you to pee in a bottle it put you off. It could take ages. For the record, I have never taken drugs. I just think it's cheating – cheating yourself and cheating everybody else in the sport who is doing it clean. I don't even like people smoking.

During the 1986–87 season, we reached two major finals: the John Player Special Trophy final at Burnden Park, Bolton and the Stones Bitter Premiership final at Old Trafford. Both times we played Wigan – and both times we lost – but we pushed them every inch of the way. Going into the final at Bolton we were the slight favourites because

44

we had won 14 games in a row and been the *Daily Mirror* team of the month for November and December. Our confidence was sky high, but so was Wigan's. A try from Henderson Gill put them 4–0 ahead before I scored in the corner to make the half-time score 4–4. A second try from Henderson Gill made it 8–4 before the turning point of the match midway through the second half. Our full-back, Brian Johnson, tried to chip the ball over Andy Goodway's head, but he caught it and ran 65 yards to score. Gill kicked the goal and then Dean Bell scored a minute from time. We had lost 18–4 in front of a big crowd, 21,144.

Going into the final at Old Trafford we were crippled by injuries. Our captain, Les Boyd, was injured. Our former captain, Ken Kelly, was injured. Our hooker, Mark Roskell, was injured. Our new stand-off, Keith Holden, was injured. And Ronnie Duane was injured. Again. Sorry Ronnie. Bob Jackson, our acting captain, had a fantastic game, but it was backs-to-the wall stuff. Joe Lydon scored a kick-and-run try for them just before half-time and Gary Sanderson had a try disallowed for us shortly after half-time. They won 8–0 in front of a Premiership record crowd of 38,756 who had braved the cold and rain.

The following weekend I played in Ken Kelly's testimonial match between Warrington Past and Warrington Present at Wilderspool. But, sadly, Ken was not able to play himself because of his knee injury, which was typical of some of the bad luck he suffered. Don't get me wrong, Ken had a wonderful career. He won the Challenge Cup with St Helens in 1972 when he was only 19. With Warrington, he won the Lancashire Cup twice and the John Player Trophy twice and was the Man of Steel and First Division Player of the Year for 1980–81. But he suffered some terrible injuries including two broken jaws and two broken arms that restricted him to just four Great Britain caps when he should have won many more. The second broken jaw, the result of a high tackle, also forced him to pull out of the Great Britain tour to Australia and New Zealand in 1979. Still, his testimonial match was a lot of fun. We – the Present – won 52–40 with Des Drummond and Bob Jackson scoring our best tries and Bob kicked a goal from the touchline. John Bevan, Eddie Hunter, Tommy Martyn, Mike Nicholas, John Fieldhouse and Reg Bowden all played for Warrington Past.

I was fast but I wasn't a particularly good trainer. I used to work in the building game and so in the summer, when that was our pre-season, it was the best time for me to get overtime to make my money up. So I always came up with an excuse to miss pre-season training, like having an ingrowing toenail. Eventually the club cottoned on to this and said: "Right, you are having your ingrowing toenail out."

I had the operation – and missed another pre-season – but the club said: "It's all right. You can do pre-season next year." But then I said I needed my tonsils out and I got away with that excuse for three years. Then the club sent me to hospital to have my tonsils out. I said: "They're all right now." But the club doctors – Dr Rothwell and Dr Scott – weren't having that and so I had to have my tonsils out. I had used up all my excuses. When I came round from the anaesthetic Gaynor said: "I can't believe you asked me to marry you." I said it didn't count because I was under anaesthetic, but I was only joking.

We got married at Warrington Parish Church in June 1987, which was out of season then, and moved into our first house in Shaws Avenue. Andy Gregory was my best man.

Left: Wedding day nerves: Mark with his best man, Andy Gregory, at St Elphin's Parish Church, Warrington, in June 1987.

Below: Mark and Gaynor leaving the Church.

(Photos: The late Stuart Ritchie)

I would never have imagined that Andy Gregory would be an organised best man, but he was. Everything with Andy tended to be off the cuff and I was thinking "This is going to be a nightmare" but come the big day he was there early and in charge of everything. He made sure the cars were right, the buttonholes were right, everything. When we watched the video later, we saw him making sure that all the aunts, uncles, grandparents and friends had got cars to the reception. He was the last to leave the church, but was still there to greet everyone at the Lymm Hotel and, obviously, he gave a very funny speech about what goes on in rugby.

My stag night had been in the Chaplin's nightclub in Warrington – people didn't go abroad for stag dos in those days. Chaplin's was owned by the Foden brothers and I have done some work for them since. I remember coming out of the club, quite squiffy, at about 1.30am. All the lads decided to strip me naked and I had to run down Mersey Street. Luckily I was fast and so not many people saw me. The lads met me at the other end of the street and gave me my clothes back. So that was another story for Andy's best man speech.

We had no money to go on a honeymoon, but the family surprised us at the wedding. They had all chipped in to send us to Lloret de Mar in Catalonia, which was one of the top holiday destinations at the time, which was very generous of them.

Our first son Christopher was born in May 1988 and Daniel followed in August 1989 but we always went out after the match on a Sunday night, which was the only time we could get a babysitter. Win, lose or draw, Gaynor and myself would go out. Some of the other players couldn't understand it. If we won, great, they would go out and want all the accolades from the fans. If we lost, they would ask why I was going out. I would say it was the only night of the week I could go out. I wasn't going to go home and sulk. I always had a rule with the supporters: don't swear or abuse me or my wife or in front of my children. If you do I will just shake your hand and politely walk away and, fair play, in my 20 years at Warrington it never happened. Supporters would say they would meet me after the game. I would say I'll be there, don't worry. If we had a good win Kelly Shelford would come along and Paul Bishop would come along, but if we lost it would just be me and Gaynor.

When the boys were growing up I bought them golf clubs, snooker cues and tennis rackets so that they wouldn't follow me into rugby league, but they did anyway. Christopher was four when he started playing the game at Bank Park on a Sunday morning with Kevin Tamati, who was the council's rugby league development officer, and my team-mate. So Kevin and I would be at Bank Park in the morning and then go and play for Warrington at Wilderspool in the afternoon. When Christopher got too old for that Gaynor and I started a junior rugby league section at the Rylands club in about 1992 with Chris Jones. Now it's a thriving section with Wayne and Carol Hewitt, Alan Brinksman, Peter Leonard and others who have joined over the years. Daniel joined Rylands as well and was in a different team. So I would watch one team one week and Gaynor would watch the other and then we would swap over. Finally, they both made it into the Rylands first team and I got this crazy idea in about 2004 to play with them. Just once. But I have lost track of the number of times I have played with them now. Both boys then decided to move over to Bank Quay Bulls and next thing Bank Quay were knocking on my door and asking me if I would be their head coach. I agreed and we are still playing together at Woolston Rovers.

Christopher is a scrum-half who has also played for Doncaster, Rochdale Hornets and Blackpool. He is a very good organiser, with a fantastic kicking game. He was named the BARLA Youth Player of the Year in 2007. Daniel is as hard as nails, an old-fashioned, cheeky hooker, and never takes a backward step. He also had the chance to join Rochdale at one time. All three of us have played for Ireland at different levels. It is strange on the pitch now. Obviously the number 7 and number 9 are two of a team's main organisers and when I am playing in the centre, second row or front row I will take the first drive at a tap penalty or a play-the-ball. The boys say "Dad, take the ball in" and the other team are in stitches. They say "Foz, are these your lads?" and I say "Yes". The other team cannot wait to get in the bar afterwards to ask the boys what it's like playing in the same side as their dad. Lots of former professionals have said they would like to do it too.

Seamus McCallion, the former Halifax hooker, played for two years in the same side as his son. After the first time, he couldn't wait to get off the pitch and tell me. He rang up and said "Foz, I've done it, I've done it". I said "What, robbed a bank, crashed your car". He said: "No, I've had a game of rugby league with my lad, now I'm retiring."

Chris is a qualified electrician and Dan is a qualified plasterer. We could almost build a house between us. My daughter, Beckie, was born in 1995. She played netball at school and a lot of people thought she would play women's rugby league but, thankfully, she hasn't. Three of us playing and getting injured is quite enough. Anyway, she always says she got fed up watching me and her two brothers play. Beckie is training to be a social worker. She makes at least one trip a year to Gambia to help the people there become self-sufficient, grow their own crops and build their own schools etc. She has also been to Romania on a similar project.

I have two grandchildren now: Taylor John Forster (Chris's son) and Maisie Lauren Forster (Dan's daughter). As a proud granddad, I put their names on the side of my van. But Beckie wasn't very happy about that, so I had to put her name on as well.

6. Great Britain debut

When the late Mike Gregory and I were called up for Great Britain as two very shy lads in January 1987, we got on the bus with Ellery Hanley, Andy Goodway, Lee Crooks, Garry Schofield, Shaun Edwards and Kevin Beardmore and they all started making animal noises. We asked "What's all that about" and were told they called Wilderspool "the zoo" because of the noise of the crowd and the front row of Les Boyd, Kevin Tamati and Bob Jackson. In fact, whoever we had in the front row was as hard as nails. After that even if we went for lunch after Great Britain training and there was bacon on the menu they would all be making squealing noises. Anything so that they could rip me and Mike Greg to bits for playing at "the zoo". But we were both picked to make our debuts against France at Headingley and, on the day before the match, had our photograph in the *Daily Mirror*, taken by the Warrington-based photographer Stuart Ritchie. We were both dressed as onion sellers, with berets, false moustaches and onions around our necks, being taught French by a model named Gillian Bell. On the big day we both scored tries and proved ourselves. Greg scored twice and I ran one in from 70 yards out as we won 52–4. We both kept our places for the return test at Carcassonne the following month and again Great Britain won, this time 20–10.

Mal Reilly, the Great Britain coach, had been a fantastic player and was a fantastic coach, probably the best I ever played under. When we played in France there was a bit of an initiation ceremony. You had to strip off and run across one lane of a dual carriageway, across a barrier and then across the other lane of the dual carriageway, around a lamppost and back. Of course, it was all right for the fast lads like Mike Greg and myself, but some of the forwards weren't quite as fit as us and not quite as fast and took a good few minutes longer. But Mal made sure we all did it. Thankfully, this was before mobile phone cameras and CCTV. It was all low key and kept in house. Mal was one of those coaches who could do anything he asked you to do. If you moaned back to him about doing 100 sit-ups or 10 press-ups, Mal could do them. He would get down on his hands and knees and do them with you.

Des Drummond was the first-choice Great Britain winger, but he was in dispute with Leigh and on the transfer list at £100,000 and so I took his shirt. Maurice Bamford, the previous Great Britain coach, had told me that if Des didn't sign for a club I would be in the squad for the tour of Australia and New Zealand the following summer. I was playing well and praying to God that Des didn't sign for anyone. One day in February 1987, on the way home from work, I saw on the *Manchester Evening News* billboard that he had signed for someone. The billboard said: "Drummond signs". I pulled over to find out who he had signed for and he had only gone and joined Warrington. Des also wanted to play on the right wing (Number 2) and so I ended up playing on the left wing (Number 5), but it didn't really matter. There wasn't much in it then, although I think it is more important now.

Great Britain 52 France 4, 24 January 1987 at Headingley

Left: Mark races in for a try against France on his Great Britain debut, and – below left – celebrates.

Below right: Mark congratulates Mike Gregory after he, too, had scored a try on his Great Britain debut against France.

(All photos: Eddie Fuller).

A winger just needed to carry the ball in the arm away from the opposition to be able to fend off tacklers. So we played on opposite wings – I was happy to play anywhere – and Des and I became great friends. Once you have been team-mates in rugby league you are team-mates forever and best mates forever.

I should have gone on the 1988 tour. In fact, not going on a Great Britain tour is probably the biggest regret of my career. It was something that everybody wanted to do for the camaraderie with the lads, but I was lucky enough to go on other tours – to Milwaukee, Fiji and the World Club Challenge. And I was lucky enough to play at Wembley and there are Great Britain tourists who did not do that – like John Woods for example.

John signed for us from Bradford Northern for £40,000 in June 1987 and what a signing he proved to be. He was an awesome player. Warrington didn't get his best years out of him, but he gave us two cracking seasons. I have never seen anyone kick goals like him. He put his heel in the ground, put the ball down, took four paces back and, bang, it went over. John was a big smoker and drinker. Whenever people wanted him, they wouldn't go to his house in Leigh, they would go to a pub, I think it was called the Foundry, where all the Leigh players went at the time. That wouldn't be allowed today. Lee Briers told me recently that none of the players – or the coaching staff – are allowed to drink alcohol anywhere inside the Halliwell Jones Stadium at any event during the season. It's a good job they didn't have that rule years ago because we all liked a drink.

With John pulling the strings, we reached the final of the Lancashire Cup against Wigan – who else – at Knowsley Road in October. Unusually, I played centre to Des Drummond, Paul Cullen must have been injured, and scored two tries in front of a crowd of 20,237, but we still lost 28–16.

We played Wigan again at Wilderspool on New Year's Day in the match that became known as 'World War Three' because four players were sent off in the opening 20 minutes. Andy Goodway flattened Paul Cullen with a high tackle and was sent off by referee Kevin Allatt. When Goodway was walking off he deliberately stood on Cull's hand. Cull jumped up, chased him down the tunnel and launched himself at Goodway and was sent off with him. Amazingly, Goodway wasn't punished for standing on Cull's hand. He should have been sent off twice really – once for the high tackle and once for standing on his hand. It was like a war. Warrington's Tony Humphries and Wigan's Adrian Shelford were also sent off and Les Boyd was put in the sin bin. All this violence erupted again when we played Wigan again in Milwaukee in June 1989.

I kicked my first goal for Warrington at Leeds in March. I only kicked three in my entire career and they were all against Leeds. I missed one from in front of the posts, but then kicked one from the touchline. I just hit it. The lads said I was the only goalkicker that they didn't want to score near the posts for. Thankfully, John Woods was back for the next match – at Wigan three days later. We won 6–2 to avenge the Lancashire Cup final defeat.

We finished sixth in the Stones Bitter Championship and so had to go to Wigan again in the first round of the Premiership. I always enjoyed playing at Central Park and scored our first try as we won 24–12 to book a semi-final at Widnes's Naughton Park, a match that brought shame on rugby league. There was a tense atmosphere from the start and it all kicked off. Players spilled off the pitch, fighting and heading towards the perimeter wall. One Widnes fan claimed that Des Drummond and some of the others had fallen on his son during the brawl. The fan marched on to the pitch to confront Dessie, who just took one step back and then punched him and put him on his backside. Dessie was charged with assault, but was cleared after stating that the fan was verbally abusing him and that he was acting in self-defence. The trouble cost Dessie his place in the Great Britain squad to tour Papua New Guinea, Australia and New Zealand that summer. He had been selected for the trip, but the Rugby Football League (RFL) withdrew his name after the police charged him. Warrington were fined a record £10,000 and, to make things worse, we lost 20–10.

This was Martin Offiah's first season in rugby league after signing for Widnes from Rosslyn Park rugby union club and, by the time of the Premiership semi-final, he had already scored 42 tries in 33 matches. Martin was on the left wing for Widnes, I was on the left wing for Warrington and Barry Peters was my centre. During the match, Martin made a break down the middle, but I turned and caught him. By this time, Barry had caught up and gave him a rabbit punch, straight on the end of the chin, and knocked him out. We both looked at each other in amazement and the referee looked at us and said: "What happened there?" We both said "We don't know" and that was it, game over for Martin. One Warrington fan was privately video recording the match and filmed the whole thing. Martin Offiah, welcome to rugby league.

That summer, Warrington signed a second-row forward called Basil Richards from the Queensbury amateur club in Bradford who thought he was a world-beater. In training he wanted to be the fastest, the best ball handler and make the biggest hits but he was fighting a losing battle with Billy McGinty, Mark Roberts and Mike Gregory all ahead of him. He was always in their shadow.

Warrington also signed two Australian Test forwards on short-term contracts, prop Steve 'Blocker' Roach from Balmain and second-row Les Davidson from South Sydney. Les Davidson was an absolute animal. I have never seen anyone tackle as hard and fierce as him. We played three games in 10 days in February and Davo injured his ribs in the first game at Hull KR. However, he didn't tell anybody because he wanted to play in the third game – against Wigan. That's how tough he was.

'Blocker' was a big unit – 6 feet 2 inches and 16 stones 7 pounds – and he came with a big reputation and so Warrington supporters expected a lot from him. Sometimes he didn't quite deliver and after one match we were in the bar at the Causeway pub having a quiet drink when this old-timer decided to give him some stick. He looked like Albert Steptoe and he must have been the best part of 75 or 80. He said: "I've taken money out of my pension to watch you and you are a load of crap." Steve took it – for a while – and then the old-timer said: "Right, I'll take you outside." Steve said OK, but I said to him: "You can't, he's 75 if he's a day." Steve reluctantly agreed and decided to buy him a pint instead. The old-timer quickly changed his tune and said that 'Blocker' wasn't such a bad player after all – and he was right. He was a good lad and a good leader. He also taught the young lads like Neil Harmon and Gary Chambers how to be better props.

That November we collected the most unusual trophy I've ever won, a miner's lamp, for winning the British Coal Nines tournament at Central Park. Again we had a mobile pack made up of Billy McGinty, Mike Gregory, Mark Roberts, John Thursfield and Gary Sanderson, who were as fast as most backs. Behind them were Dave Lyon, Brian Carbert, Ronnie Duane, Rocky Turner, John Woods and myself. We did it the hard way too, beating Wigan and St Helens on the way to the final, and the Rest of the World in the final itself. We weren't the favourites because Wigan were winning everything at the time and were at home and so we had nothing to lose. The Rest of the World team was full of Australians, Kiwis and Papua New Guineans, basically anyone who was like lightning. John Woods was the man of the tournament.

Ten days after we'd won the British Coal Nines, Warrington coach Tony Barrow stunned us all by quitting in the changing room at Wilderspool after we had beaten Oldham 21–14 in the first round of the John Player Special Trophy. There was a feeling in the game that clubs had to have an Australian coach if they wanted to win something and maybe if they wanted to sign the best Australian players. Tony felt his position was under threat. He was a man of his word and he resigned.

No disrespect to Tony, but a lot of people in Australia hadn't heard of him while everybody in rugby league had heard of Les Boyd. Warrington offered the job to Les, but he turned it down for business reasons and Brian Johnson was appointed instead. Tony was appointed as the Oldham coach the following week.

Clive Griffiths had one game in charge as Warrington's caretaker coach – Leeds away – and we won 22–8. We were leading 16–8 inside the last 10 minutes and Leeds were launching attack after attack. Cliff Lyons, their Australian stand-off, attempted a long pass but I intercepted it and ran 75 yards to score, with Andrew Ettingshausen in hot pursuit. I had beaten ET, as Ettingshausen was known, in the fastest man in rugby league competition two years earlier, but he had complained that he was carrying an injury. So it was very pleasing to beat him again. Clive was my friend for life after that. As a coach, Clive was ahead of his time. He was very clever and tactically aware and liked to give his players free rein.

Warrington 42 Bramley 10
Sunday 27 November 1988, John Player Trophy, second round
This was Brian Johnson's first game as Warrington coach and I was obviously trying to make a good impression. I scored in the first five minutes but after 10 minutes I had broken my leg. I was just running down the pitch, hit a divot and my tibia snapped, with the ligaments torn from the bone. It was as simple as that. I was carried off on a stretcher and put straight into an ambulance and taken to hospital. The ambulance men wound the window down so that I could hear the cheers from the crowd as we went over Bridge Foot.

I said: "Thanks a lot for that lads." I think they were just trying to keep my mind off the pain. I was in plaster for two months and out for four months.

Injuries are part and parcel of the game, but this one meant that I missed the match at Naughton Park in March 1989 when Martin Offiah scored five tries against Warrington for Widnes. Des Drummond and Paul Williamson were the Warrington wingers that day. Not me[1]. But I also missed out on the Challenge Cup semi-final against Wigan at Maine Road when Joe Lydon broke Warrington hearts by kicking a drop-goal from 61 yards. Steve Roach was flown back from Australia and had his best game for the club. He always said the problem was that when he played with a young prop, like Tony Humphries or Steve Molloy, the opposition just concentrated on him and not the young lad. He was playing against two props. In the semi-final, his other prop was Les Boyd and so he could show what he could really do.

---

[1] Martin Offiah wasn't the first player to score five tries against Warrington. I am reliably informed – by Gary – that that honour goes to Ike Southward, the former Great Britain winger, who scored five tries for Workington Town against Warrington at Derwent Park in January 1959. Not many people know that.

Mark heading for the posts for a try at Wigan in April 1988,
leaving Mark Preston and Joe Lydon in his wake.

John Woods about to touch down against Widnes at Naughton Park in May 1988.
(Both photos: Eddie Fuller)

55

Warrington versus Hull, September 1988. Left to right, back: Les Davidson, Gary Sanderson, Dave Lyon, coach Tony Barrow, Mark Roberts, Neil Harmon, Steve Roach, Tony Humphries, Mike Gregory; front: Barry Peters, Paul Bishop, Mark Roskell, Des Drummond, John Woods, Paul Cullen, Phil Blake, Mark Forster. (Photo: Eddie Fuller)

Left: Caretaker coach Clive Griffiths guided Warrington to a 22–8 victory at Leeds in November 1988. (Photo courtesy Gary Slater)

Right: Mark leaves a Bramley player in touch as he heads for the posts at Wilderspool in November 1988 during Brian Johnson's first game as coach. Minutes later Mark broke his leg. (Photo: Eddie Fuller)

7. Milwaukee and Wembley

In the summer of 1989 Warrington and Wigan went to America to play an American Challenge match at the Milwaukee County Stadium in Wisconsin. Most of us had never been to America before and we were really looking forward to it. This was in the days before proper sponsorship and Warrington forgot to buy tracksuits for the journey and so, at the last minute, the kit man was sent to Warrington Market to get some. He bought the cheapest shell suits he could find. The tops were too big, the bottoms were too small. No club badge. We looked an absolute mess and when we got to Manchester Airport and Wigan arrived they had everything – or rather two of everything: baseball caps, T-shirts, vests, track suits, all with a Milwaukee badge. They all had the same make of trainers. In comparison, we looked like a pub side.

We stopped in Chicago for two nights to promote the game and stayed in a really dodgy place. We had to go to the toilet in groups of three or four great big rugby players, down an escalator and along a dark corridor. We were glad to get to Milwaukee, where we were greeted by a ticker-tape parade, which was absolutely fantastic. We went to training in a yellow bus, like on *The Simpsons*, and the driver left the keys in the ignition and Kevin Tamati decided to steal it, with all the players on board. We had a drive around the car park and came back and Kevin got his arse kicked. But it was a great laugh and brought everybody down to earth.

The Warrington wingers were Des Drummond and me; they had Joe Lydon and Mark Preston. When we saw the pitch we found that the baseball diamond was in one of the corners. We all said 'we aren't playing and diving on that'. They made the pitch shorter and narrower which, we thought, would suit Warrington, but it didn't quite work out that way.

Wigan 12 Warrington 5
Saturday 10 June 1989, The American Challenge Match, Milwaukee County Stadium
Les Boyd didn't particularly like Ellery Hanley and Ellery didn't particularly like Les Boyd. But the RFL, in their infinite wisdom, flew them both in from Sydney – where Ellery was playing for Balmain at the time – and decided to sit them next to each other on the 15-hour flight. They didn't speak to each other at all, just let out the occasional grunt. They arrived in Milwaukee the night before us, because we were still in Chicago, but the RFL hadn't booked them a room and so they had to share an 8 feet by 8 feet office. They were still not speaking to each other. When game day arrived the tension between them exploded just 87 seconds into the match. It was one of the fiercest fights ever. All hell broke loose, with Les, Ellery, Mike Gregory and Andy Gregory all involved on a narrow pitch.

John Holdsworth from Kippax was the referee and he was right in the middle of them. He was mic-ed up because it was an exhibition game and he was calling them by their names and pulling them out and pushing them away. The video of the match is absolutely fantastic, but I can't imagine any of today's referees getting involved in that way, but John did. Not surprisingly, he sent Les and Ellery to the sin bin. Later on, I drove the ball in and one Wigan player tackled me around the legs and on the way down I collided with Ian Lucas's knee and was knocked out completely. When I came round, I didn't know where I was and ended up sitting on the bench. A few of the lads and myself had arranged to go to Miami after the match for a week's holiday but the doctor said I couldn't go. I had to go back to England for scans on my neck to see what damage I had done. So Ian Lucas's knee cost me a week in Miami with the lads.

But I did get one memorable night out in Milwaukee with Ronnie Duane and John Woods. We found a little bar, not far from the hotel, and John ordered three pints. The bar man said he could have the three pints for his tie. John didn't collect ties and so he agreed. Next time it was John's round the bar man said he could have the three pints for his jumper. John didn't collect jumpers either and so again he agreed. Next time it was John's round – and by this time we were getting a bit squiffy after six pints – the bar man said he could have the three pints for his shirt. By now, Ronnie and I had sussed out what was going on – but we hadn't told John – we were actually in a gay bar and the bar staff were undressing him. He never lived that down. He got his gear back and the three of us walked very briskly back to the coach. Ronnie and I told the rest of the players what had happened and John Woods got ripped to bits by them.

Also that summer Warrington signed another winger, David Myers, from Widnes, but he did not really settle at Wilderspool. He was big and strong; the lads used to call him 'Fatty' Myers but there wasn't much fat on him. He was just strong. He moved on to Wigan in 1990 and went on the Great Britain tour of Australia and New Zealand in 1992. David was another one who died too soon. He was killed in a car crash on the M6 in October 2008 after suffering a heart attack. He was just 37.

The 1989–90 season was Brian Johnson's first full campaign as Warrington coach and turned out to be a great success, despite us selling stand-off John Woods to Rochdale Hornets for £50,000 before a ball had even been kicked. We thrashed Wigan 42–16 in the Locker Cup game at Wilderspool. I scored a hat-trick to win the Ernie Ashcroft Shield as man-of-the-match. Confidence was sky high and we beat Wigan again, 18–6 at Central Park, on the opening day of the season. Johnno had signed an Australian scrum-half, Greg Mackey, and he made his debut in that game, facing Wigan's Andy Gregory. We won our first six games before drawing 12–12 with Hull and then came the ultimate test, playing Widnes – the newly-crowned world club champions – at Wilderspool in a Lancashire Cup semi-final. In the changing room before kick-off Tony Thorniley was not happy with his boots and borrowed a pair from our injured second-row forward Mark Roberts. It was not ideal, but it worked. Tony scored two tries, I scored one and we won 28–6.

Warrington 24 Oldham 16
Saturday 14 October 1989, Lancashire Cup final, Knowsley Road
This was my third Lancashire Cup final after the defeats of 1985 and 1987 and it was fantastic to finally win one. I scored a try in the corner and could have had a hat-trick – but

for Bob Jackson. Bob was back in the team after missing a season through injury and going back home to Australia to recover. He was still getting his match fitness back. Twice in the second half, Bob drifted over towards my wing for a rest and both times he got the ball and went over for tries that should have been mine. He was named the man-of-the-match as well. But none of that mattered because we had won a trophy.

That November, Warrington signed two New Zealand internationals – centre Gary Mercer and hooker Duane Mann – who were on tour with the Kiwis. Their first taste of life with the Wire was a boot camp at Llanberis in Snowdonia in North Wales.

We had to move sheep off the field before we could train and Gary Mercer, who had arrived wearing an immaculate white coat, said: "What on earth have I joined Warrington for? I could have stopped in New Zealand for this."

Mark Roberts and Billy McGinty were the practical jokers in the squad, the gruesome twosome, always playing tricks in the dressing room or on the team coach, hiding gear, switching underwear and T-shirts, that sort of thing. At Llanberis, they set the fire alarms off in the middle of the night and so we decided we would get them back. We filled Mark Roberts' trainers with tomato sauce, brown sauce and mayonnaise. But Robbo was a diabetic and he had hidden all his blood testing equipment and insulin in his trainers and had to be rushed to the doctors.

So that was a practical joke that backfired and we had to start behaving after that. But we did balance cups of water on top of doors so that when Billy and Robbo came through they would get soaked. Unfortunately, Brian Johnson was walking about at the time and got drenched by three different doors.

Gary Mercer and Duane Mann were two of the first players to have club cars. After training with them we couldn't find our cars because one of those two had driven their car against one of ours and pushed it to the far end of the car park.

St Helens 0 Warrington 0
Wednesday 28 February 1990, Stones Bitter Championship
This match was abandoned after four minutes when a corrugated panel from the main stand blew loose and landed a few feet away from me and Gary Mercer. I was on the wing and Gary was in the centre and the panel landed in between us. A few feet either way and it would have killed one of us. If I had been a cat I would have used up one of my nine lives that night and I had used up some already.

Our luck had held in the Challenge Cup as well with home ties against Featherstone Rovers and Trafford Borough in the first two rounds. The tie against Featherstone, who were also in the First Division, was shown on television on BBC's *Grandstand*. We built up a 17–0 lead by half-time with tries from Mike Gregory and Billy McGinty to have the tie won. Featherstone had a right good go at the start of the second half and closed the gap to 17–12, but we held on to win 20–12.

1989 Locker Cup

Left: Mark scores one of his three tries against Wigan at Wilderspool.

Below: Paul Cullen reaches for a drink after the match. Also shown, left to right, back: Rocky Turner, Bob Jackson, Basil Richards; front: Mike Bacon, Tony Burke, Mark Forster.

(Both photos: Eddie Fuller)

1989 Lancashire Cup Final

Mark scores against Oldham at Central Park in the 1989 Lancashire Cup Final.

Lancashire Cup winners 1989 in the changing room: Left to right, back: Mark Forster, Rocky Turner, Mark Roskell, Tony Burke, Steve Molloy, Gary Sanderson; front: Paul Darbyshire, Greg Mackey, Tony Thorniley, Mike Gregory, David Lyon, Ronnie Duane. (Both photos: Eddie Fuller).

We were losing 7–6 to Trafford Borough at half-time, but stepped it up in the second half to win 20–12 with Tony Thorniley scoring two tries and Paul Bishop and me one each.

The draw for the third round, the quarter-finals, could hardly have been tougher – Bradford away – but our forwards were magnificent and helped us to win 12–10. Bob Jackson scored our only try and Rocky Turner kicked four goals to earn himself a "Rocky IV" headline in one of the local papers.

Wigan beat St Helens in the first semi-final at Old Trafford, leaving us to face Second Division Oldham in the second semi-final at Central Park three weeks later. We were the favourites, but the problem was that Tony Barrow, the former Warrington coach, was now in charge of Oldham and knew all about us. There was another problem too. Paul Bishop, our first-choice scrum-half, fell downstairs on the morning of the match and put his arm through a pane of glass, cutting his arm. He couldn't play and so Brian Johnson had to find the 'A' team scrum-half Martin Crompton, who was walking to the match from his home in Wigan, eating a ham sandwich.

After all that, Oldham took the lead and held on to it until the second half before Martin scored a try and then, with time running out, I crossed at the corner. In total, I scored 191 tries for Warrington, but that was the best and most important. Warrington had not been to Wembley since 1975, but we had won 10–6 and were going back to the Twin Towers after a gap of 15 years. Martin and I had our picture taken together in the dressing room afterwards. It is one of my favourite photographs.

Tony Barrow saw me in the bar afterwards and clipped me around the ear and said: "I can't believe you have done that to me after I've looked after you all these years." He had a jovial go at me and then congratulated me on getting to Wembley. He said I took the chance well. If he couldn't get to Wembley, he wanted it to be one of his boys who did.

After that there was a massive build-up to the final itself. Most of us were working full-time, but the companies we worked for were quite happy because they were getting a lot of publicity. We did a lot of promotions. Basically, what they do all the time now, we did for Wembley week.

We trained and did different promotions on the Monday and the Tuesday, played golf at Walton Hall on the Wednesday and then travelled down on the Thursday. All except Steve Molloy that is. Steve had played in all four cup ties on the road to Wembley, but Brian Johnson dropped him for the final itself. He was furious and never played for Warrington again. He was sold to Leeds for £110,000 that September.

But he still went to the final and sat with the fans. When the final hooter sounded Steve decided he wanted to be with the lads on the pitch and so he climbed over the fence. One of the stewards saw him and thought about stopping him. Then he saw the size of Steve – and the look in his eyes – and decided not to bother. We thought he was going to have a go at Brian Johnson, but he wasn't. He just wanted to congratulate the lads.

Mark scored in the corner against Oldham in the 1990 Challenge Cup semi–final at Central Park to take Warrington back to Wembley for the first time in 15 years.

Mark and Martin Crompton in the changing room after the Challenge Cup semi–final victory. Both players scored tries that day.

(Both photos: Eddie Fuller)

Warrington 14 Wigan 36

Saturday 28 April 1990, Challenge Cup Final, Wembley

My shoulder had popped out three times in the match before Wembley, but kept popping back in and so I never told anyone. But it dislocated completely during the final. Tony Rothwell, the physio, told me to come off the field. I said: "No way. It's taken me 10 years to get here and I'm not coming off." So he actually put the shoulder back in on the pitch at Wembley. By this time the BBC had zoomed in to see what was happening and my face is a picture: the screaming, the agony and the bad language. I ran off and carried on playing. Unfortunately, we lost and I went up the 39 steps to collect my medal and did a lap of honour. By now I was in so much pain I didn't really know where I was. I saw a close friend – Wayne Buckles, who was known as Wan – in the crowd and asked him: "What are you doing here?" He answered: "We're at Wembley, there's 80,000 of us and we've come to watch you play." "Oh, all right," I said. He still reminds me of that to this day.

When I finished the lap of honour the surgeon was waiting for me and he said: "Come on Foz, what have you done?" He took a look at the shoulder and said: "We'll operate on that tomorrow." "No you won't," I told him. "We've got the open top bus tour back in Warrington and then all the lads will be celebrating for two or three days." He operated on me a week and a half later, put the shoulder back in place and I was out for eight months. During that time I lost two stones in weight because they strapped my arm up in protective padding that was 35mm thick. It was summer and I was constantly sweating, but I was able to do leg weights.

I was back in full training with the first team in December and the lads beat Widnes 8–4 in the Regal Trophy semi-final at Central Park on Saturday 29th. It was a brilliant result and both the wingers, Des Drummond and Paul Williamson, played really well and so I was sure that I wouldn't be playing at Wigan on New Year's Day, even though Brian Johnson had called me into the squad. So, for the first time ever, I went out on New Year's Eve in the Touchdown club at Wilderspool until four in the morning. I went to Wigan and had a shower, because I was stinking of ale, and then Brian Johnson told me I was playing. I pleaded with him not to change a winning team, but it was no good. I was playing in front of 15,916 fans at Central Park.

When I went out for the warm-up a ripple went around the crowd: "He was in the club until four o'clock." It seemed like everybody was pointing at me. The first 20 minutes seemed to last forever as I struggled with my hangover but, midway through the half, I started to come round a little bit. My eyes were starting to focus properly and Wigan were attacking the far end away from the tunnel. I saw the ball come across and there was a cracking pass from Dean Bell to Mark Preston. I intercepted it and ran the full length of the field to score. It was my first game for eight months and when I touched down I was absolutely exhausted. Gary Chambers said that once I caught the ball no one was going to catch me and I wasn't going to pass to anyone and so there was no point in following me. I told him I didn't need someone to pass to, I needed someone to carry me back. We won 14–6 and some fans said I could go out drinking until 4am before every match.

Left: Mark sets off for an interception try in the Premiership Trophy game at Wigan in April 1990.

Bottom left: Mark Forster prepares to touch down at Wigan despite the best efforts of Mark Preston (left) to catch him.

Above: Another try against Wigan in the same match.

(All photos: Eddie Fuller)

It is very satisfying when you have scored a try – especially a full length of the field try – and helped your team to win. I scored something like seven interception tries against Wigan during my career and the Wigan boys used to say that Dean Bell gave better passes to me that he did to his own wingers.

While I was injured Warrington had signed a new stand-off, an angry little Australian from Canberra Raiders called Chris O'Sullivan. Like Napoleon, we thought he had little man syndrome. During his time at Wilderspool, he picked two fights, one with Kurt Sorensen and one with Emosi Koloto, two giant Widnes forwards. Emosi was about 7 feet 2 inches and Kurt knocked players down for fun, but Sully wanted to fight both of them that day and he never took a backwards step. He had great footwork and great skills, but wasn't quite the stature of player we were expecting.

Warrington had also signed two Welsh rugby union internationals in centre Allan Bateman and flanker Rowland Phillips, both from Neath. It was always easier for backs to switch codes than forwards and Allan went on to play for Great Britain. He was an amazing tackler. He made some great breaks and half-breaks for me and I would finish them off. Rowland, on the other hand, signed as a flanker – and there are no flankers in rugby league – and so ended up in the front row. He was a big unit and a lot was expected from him, but he didn't quite make it at Warrington.

We played Bradford Northern at Headingley in the Regal Trophy final, but Dave Lyon, our full-back and goalkicker, was a doubt all week with an eye injury and so I trained all week as a goalkicker and full-back. I was very glad when he made it and kicked four goals to help us win a dour match 12–2. Substitute Mark Thomas scored our only try in the last minute and Billy McGinty won the man-of-the-match award after a non-stop performance in the second row. Billy was a great player, but he was under-estimated until he joined Wigan for £60,000 in August 1991. Wigan were full-time professionals while we were part-time and, with all the full-time training, he went up three collar sizes. At Wigan, of course, he became famous for the "pineapple ring" story after the 1992 Challenge Cup final at Wembley. John Major, the then Prime Minister, went into the changing rooms to congratulate the Wigan players after their victory over Castleford just as Billy was emerging naked from the showers except for a yellow ring around his manhood.

The PM, no doubt shocked and stunned, wondered if it was a pineapple ring. In fact, it wasn't. It was a circle of yellow padding that Billy wore to protect his knee, but that has gone down in rugby league folklore as the "pineapple ring final". Typical Billy. He also played for Workington Town, went on tour with Great Britain in 1992 and coached Scotland – twice – before switching codes. In 2011 he was appointed Edinburgh's defence coach before, in 2013, he joined the coaching set-up at the Royal Grammar School in Worcester.

Warrington 22 Huddersfield 4
Sunday 27 January 1991, Challenge Cup, preliminary round
This was my 200th game for Warrington and I was hoping to celebrate with a try. Instead I was carried off on a stretcher after a kick in the head that needed seven stitches.

1991 Regal Trophy winners

Des Drummond collects the Regal Trophy after the victory over Bradford Northern in the final at Headingley in January 1991. David Lyon is next in line. (Photo: Eddie Fuller)

Warrington players celebrate with the Regal Trophy after their next home game. Left to right, back: Rowland Phillips, Duane Mann, Chris Rudd, Gary Chambers, Allan Bateman, Gary Mercer, Dave Lyon, Mark Thomas, Paul Cullen; front: Neil Harmon, Billy McGinty, Des Drummond (captain), Kevin Ellis and Mark Forster. Tony Thorniley is missing from the Regal Trophy–winning side. (Photo: Gary Skentelbery / *Warrington Worldwide*)

St Helens 62 Warrington 16
Sunday 14 April 1991, Stones Bitter Championship

This was another nightmare afternoon at Knowsley Road. One of the St Helens players – I have decided not to name him – gouged me and I was livid. I could only see out of one eye. Gouging has no place in rugby. We were only part-time players with full-time jobs and needed our eyesight to earn a living. Jonathan Griffiths, the St Helens stand-off, kicked ahead and I wiped him out with a late tackle. Dave Carter, the referee, sent me off. We were already losing 18–0 and went on to lose 62–16 – our heaviest defeat for 63 years. Alan Hunte scored four tries for St Helens. It was our last game of a long season and proved to be a match too far. I was banned for four matches and so missed the start of the next season. Once my suspension was over, Brian Johnson made me play for the Wizards, the 'A' team, for four matches to punish me and to get my sharpness back. Finally, seven months after the St Helens game, I was back in the first team for the visit of Leeds in the Regal Trophy. We were the holders and the television cameras would be there. Bring it on!

Warrington 8 Leeds 17
Saturday 16 November 1991, Regal Trophy first round

Sadly, my timing was still a bit out. I moved in to tackle Morvin Edwards, the Leeds full-back, but it was muddy and I slipped. Unfortunately, I caught him under the chin. He went down like the proverbial sack of spuds, his gum shield flew into the Fletcher End, 20 yards away, and he was carried off on a stretcher. I got another early bath, but I waited for him before walking off to make sure he was all right. He actually got off the stretcher and walked down the tunnel, down the eight steps, along the bottom and then up the other eight steps to get into the dressing room. He was OK. I said: "Morvin, are you going back on? You have got my career in your hands here. Please go back on to prove you're OK." He said: "No, Foz, it's too cold out there. I'm a Kiwi." The tackle looked terrible and was shown over and over again on television. I went back to Red Hall and sat in the same chair I'd been in only seven months earlier. It was more bad publicity for the game and I was hit with an eight-match ban. In my last two first team games I had been sent off twice and banned for 12 matches. Anybody would think I was Mike Nicholas or Big Jim Mills.

The Leeds match was the first time I had played – albeit briefly – with our new signing from New Zealand, stand-off Kelly Shelford. He was a cracking lad but a bit of a mystery as well. A few years later his wife, Sharon, tried to organise a surprise 30th birthday party for him. Kelly found out about it and said: "You can't have a surprise 30th because I'm actually 32." Even his wife didn't know his real age. Kelly had great footwork and his hands were probably faster than his feet, but he wasn't the best of trainers because he knew he could just turn up on the day and get the job done. Players like that must be the bane of coaches' lives.

On another occasion, Kelly, Sharon, Gaynor and myself got into a bit of a scrape involving the mayor's car. We had all been to a club function at the Parr Hall but, afterwards, we couldn't get a taxi. At this point "Ed 1" – the black Daimler used by the

Mayor of Warrington – turned up. The Mayor that year was Mike Hannon, who was a bricklayer by trade and who I knew quite well, and so I decided to push my luck and ask for a lift home in his car. Mike said it was OK if John, the driver, didn't mind and as long as we were discreet about it. So that was all agreed, except we didn't ask John to take us home, we asked him to take us to the Mississippi Showboat nightclub instead. When we arrived there was a large crowd of people outside and everybody moved out of the way because they thought the Mayor was coming. We four got out of the car, staggered a little bit, and everyone fell about laughing. Sorry Mike.

While he was at Warrington, Kelly bought a British bulldog called Rollie and was going to take it back to New Zealand with him and breed it over there, but he had forgotten about the quarantine laws and the cost of transporting a dog 11,000 miles. So when Kelly finally returned to New Zealand around 1997 I got a phone call from the *Warrington Guardian* saying that he had left Rollie behind in Staffordshire and that if nobody came to claim him he would be put down. My kids all knew Rollie and liked him and so we adopted him. He became a Forster.

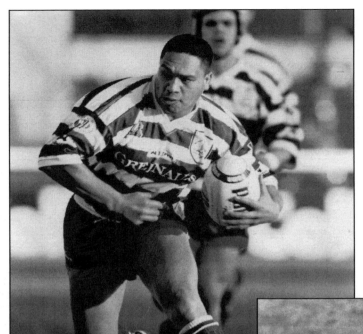

Left: Mystery Man! Even Kelly Shelford's wife wasn't sure how old he was.
(Photo: courtesy Gary Slater)

Below: Paul Cullen made 350 appearances for Warrington from 1981 to 1996 and was first–team coach from 2002 to 2008.
(Photo: Eddie Fuller)

8. A nightmare year

I was looking forward to 1992, it was my first testimonial year, but to be honest it turned into a bit of a nightmare on and off the pitch. To start with, I was still suspended from the Morvin Edwards episode and did not play for the first team until March which was unbelievably frustrating. I was 27 years old and desperate to play. I only started nine games in the 1991–92 season.

Then, in early July, we returned from a wonderful family holiday in Majorca only to find out that our home in Shaws Avenue in Orford had been broken into. To make matters worse, we were in the process of moving to Cleveleys Road in Penketh. The moving date had been put back a week, but everything was boxed up and packed with writing on the side of the boxes ready to go. The thieves must have thought all their Christmases had come at once. They didn't even have to look for things. They just had to pick up the boxes and walk out with them. It was around the time of Warrington Walking Day and a lot of the police blamed the fairground people who set up at Orford Park. We lost a portable television set, a microwave oven, other electrical goods and, worst of all, my rugby memorabilia. All my medals were stolen, including my Wembley medal, and Wembley shirt. The *Warrington Guardian* carried the story. I said that I wasn't too bothered about the electrical goods, they could be replaced, but my Wembley medal and shirt were irreplaceable. My friends also put the word out.

Twenty-four hours later, all my medals and jumpers were folded up and stacked nice and neatly on my front door step. So burglars must read the *Warrington Guardian*. After we moved we still kept in touch with friends in Shaws Avenue and were told that exactly one year later, to the week, the house was burgled again. The police said that was quite common. The burglars know that you have got a new television and a new microwave and, after a year has passed, you have dropped your guard, thinking you are safe.

We were told about our break-in on the way back from Manchester Airport and we were also told some more bad news. Gaynor's 12-year-old cousin, David Higginson, from Grappenhall, had died on a Scouting trip to Snowdonia. He had fallen 1,300ft down a mountainside at Nant Gwynant and died of his injuries.

Next, I missed the first two months of the 1992–93 season after having an operation to remove an ingrowing toenail and, unbelievably, some of my testimonial money was stolen during a burglary at Wilderspool. At the time, I had a club car, a white Ford Orion, which was a very popular make, but it was a very unlucky car. We had a testimonial quiz at the Causeway pub on Wilderspool Causeway on my birthday, 25 November. I was given a birthday cake and cards and presents and we made some money from the quiz.

Driving back to Penketh, we stopped at the Bowling Green pub, where I had arranged a dinner the following week. It was raining; we parked right outside and ran into the pub. We came out half a pint later to find that the car had been stolen. There was just a dry patch on the ground where the car had been. It turned up in Huyton 18 minutes later.

They must have raced through every red light and over every speed bump. They stamped on the birthday cake, pinched the presents and ripped up testimonial brochures. The money was gone, there was £1,000 worth of damage to the car and the radio was broken.

The Ford dealers said I could still use the car but, obviously, the radio wouldn't work. A few days later I was driving around the Crosfields roundabout, next to the Bowling Green pub, when sparks started coming out from underneath the car and it caught fire. I rang Warrington and Ron Close, the club secretary, answered. I said: "Ron, do you know anyone who puts fires out?" He said: "What are you up to now Foz? You are always messing about." This was before everyone had mobile phones and I was in a telephone box, watching the car go up in flames. I told him my club car was on fire and he still didn't believe me, but at least I got a new club car out of it.

Through it all the testimonial committee, chaired by the marvellous Mrs Evelyn McEvoy, worked their socks off. There was a New Year's Eve Party at the Touchdown club and a sports dinner at the Fir Grove Hotel in Grappenhall in January 1993 to round things off. At the dinner I was presented with a cheque for £20,000 – a percentage of which I donated to the children's ward at Warrington District General Hospital. Evelyn, who sadly died in 2015, was the life and soul of the party. She once knitted a jumper with Mike Gregory's name on the front and my name on the back. I asked why I was on the back and she said she wanted to see Mike Gregory in the mirror every morning.

But my own disappointments were put into perspective on Saturday 20 March 1993 when two IRA bombs exploded in Warrington town centre killing two boys – three-year-old Jonathan Ball and 12-year-old Tim Parry. I was working on Hallfields Road in Orford at the time, putting up a fence with two other joiners and we heard the sirens. Then everybody was walking back from town, crying and screaming. It was a sad day for Warrington. It was the day before Mother's Day and Christopher and Daniel were going to go into town with Gaynor's cousin to buy cards. Thankfully, something delayed them or they might have been near McDonald's where a bomb went off. Gaynor never got a card that year, but it didn't matter. Our boys were safe. There was a minute's silence before the next home game, against St Helens, and it was one of the most emotional ones I have ever been involved in. Every fan was silent. There was also a ground collection at Wilderspool that raised a record amount. I met Tim Parry's mum and dad, Wendy and Colin, about four or five weeks later at a Warrington Sports Personality dinner. They were there as guests of the *Warrington Guardian*. I was amazed at how calm and composed they were.

As I mentioned before, I luckily missed the match in March 1989 when Martin Offiah scored five tries against Warrington for Widnes. I was not so fortunate in April 1993 when he repeated the feat and scored five against Warrington for Wigan. Wigan then were the Great Britain side – Shaun Edwards, Steve Hampson, Jason Robinson, Joe Lydon, Denis Betts, Andy Farrell, Phil Clarke and Andy Platt – plus Frano Botica and Dean Bell. They were beating everybody. Three of Martin's tries were due to his blistering pace, the other two were given to him on a plate. He scored 10 tries for Wigan against Leeds in a Premiership Trophy semi-final in 1992. That was just embarrassing for the Leeds wingers.

Scoring a try against Leeds at Wilderspool in the Premiership in April 1992.
Kevin Ellis keeps Carl Gibson at bay. (Both photos: Eddie Fuller)

73

Mark scoops up a loose ball against Bradford Northern at Wilderspool in October 1992, watched by Rick Thackray. (Photo: Eddie Whitham)

Left: The little general, Greg Mackey, rejoined Warrington for the 1992–93 season.

(Photo: courtesy Gary Slater)

9. Champions for 19 hours

Every time I had a fall-out with the coach or the chairman they put me on the transfer list to teach me a lesson. In December 1987 they put me on the list with an asking price of £85,000. Then, in July 1989, they reduced the fee to £40,000. Nothing happened and I carried on playing for Warrington and scoring tries. I remember coming home from work down Wilderspool Causeway one day in June 1993, past the newsagents and the *Manchester Evening News* billboard said "Wire stars for sale". I stopped to see who was on the list and opened the paper to find out that I was for sale. The club hadn't told me.

Fourteen players were listed for a total of £350,000: Neil Harmon at £95,000, Tony Thorniley £65,000, the late Neil Kenyon £45,000, Duane Mann £25,000, Gary Tees £25,000, Robert 'Rocky' Turner £25,000, Basil Richards £20,000, me £15,000, Des Drummond £10,000, Mike Bacon, Ian Percival, Mark Thomas, John Westhead and Don Duffy all £5,000.

This time I came close to leaving. Peter Walsh was the Workington coach; they were signing players and giving them houses and cars. He was going to treble the money Warrington were offering and so, obviously, I was interested. But I was always late getting to Wilderspool so don't know why I thought I could get to Workington. I got on the M6 to go and meet him. I got as far as the Tickled Trout exit at Preston. That took me about two hours in the traffic. I pulled off the motorway, rang him and said: "Peter, I can't be doing this every day." I turned round, went straight to Wilderspool and signed for Warrington again. I was glad I did because in July we signed Jonathan Davies from Widnes.

The following month we signed an Australian prop named Craig Teitzel and the headlines in the *Warrington Guardian* promised that the 'Mad Butcher' was coming to town. We were all thinking they had signed another crackpot like Les Boyd, Steve Roach and Les Davidson. But when he arrived he was more 'gentle giant' than "Mad Butcher". One night, we went to a *Rocky Horror* theme show at Warrington Cricket Club and Craig was dressed in a basque and suspenders and we asked him why he was called the 'Mad Butcher'. Craig said he was actually a butcher by trade and so the *Warrington Guardian* was half right.

Jonathan Davies was 30 – two years older than me – and was coming to the end of his career, but he was still a fantastic player. I never really knew what he was going to do next and I don't think he did, but it worked. That first season, 1993–94, he played 30 matches and scored 21 tries and kicked 110 goals, including 11 drop-goals. He was the Man of Steel and the First Division Player of the Year.

One of his first games was against Halifax at Wilderspool on a Monday night in October and is best remembered because the floodlights failed. The score was at 6–6 after nine minutes of the second half when the lights went out – shortly after Jiffy had knocked on. The players had to leave the field. Announcer Peter Robinson put out an appeal for an electrician while his assistant, Phil Shaw, played "Always look on the bright side of life".

1993 Locker Cup win

Mike Gregory celebrates a try against Wigan in the Locker Cup on his return from injury in August 1993. (Photo: Eddie Whitham)

Locker Cup winners 1993: Left to right, back: Rowland Phillips, Tony Thorniley, Robert Myler, Gary Sanderson, John Thursfield, Andy Bennett, Paul Williamson, Paul Cullen, Mark Forster, Mark Hilton: front: Steve Griffiths, Lee Penny, captain Mike Gregory, Bob Jackson, Kevin Ellis, Kelly Shelford, Gary Chambers. (Photo: Eddie Fuller)

Left: Jonathan Davies made 66 appearances for Warrington from 1993 to 1995, scoring 43 tries and kicking 232 goals plus 26 drop goals.
(Photo: courtesy Gary Slater)

Below: Mark jumps for a high ball against Bradford at Wilderspool in October 1993.
(Photo: Eddie Whitham)

After 24 minutes, the lights came back on and Jonathan scored a try, two penalties and a drop goal to win us the match 15–7. The game ended at 10.04pm.

We won 14 of our first 18 matches and Wigan must have been worried because at the end of December they signed the All Black superstar Va'aiga Tuigamala – Inga the Winger – on a four-year contract worth £350,000. Two weeks later I scored a hat-trick in 18 minutes against Leeds at Wilderspool. The headline in the *Warrington Guardian* linked the two stories together: "Who needs Inga the Winger? We've got Forster the flyer!" Nice one.

Also in January, Jonathan Davies scored two amazing tries in 12 minutes in front of the *Grandstand* cameras in the fourth round of the Challenge Cup. We were losing 12–4 at Halifax at half-time, but Jonathan's tries helped us to win 22–18. He had blistering pace off the mark. He also took us to the brink of the title. Going into the final weekend we were level on points with Wigan and Bradford Northern with one match left to play.

We played Sheffield Eagles at Wilderspool on the Friday night and, with the crowd going crazy, won 36–18 with tries from Greg Mackey, Rowland Phillips, Iestyn Harris, Jonathan Davies, Allan Bateman and Jon Roper. Jonathan kicked five goals while Greg Mackey and Allan Bateman both kicked drop-goals. We had done our bit and we met up at the Red Lion pub in Stockton Heath on the Saturday afternoon to watch Leeds play Bradford at Headingley. Leeds were in the Challenge Cup Final against Wigan the following week, fielded a weakened team and Bradford annihilated them 52–10. We sat and watched as our dreams of winning the league floated away. Leeds were later fined for fielding a weakened team. Wigan then thrashed Oldham 50–6 on the Sunday to win the title and leave us in third place on points difference, but we had been champions for 19 hours.

Of course, all Warrington fans know the match – and refereeing mistake – that really cost us the title. That was against Wigan at Wilderspool on Sunday 2 January in front of a crowd of 11,379 with 2,000 fans locked out. I scored our try and three minutes into injury time, with only 10 seconds to go, the score was 6–6 and then disaster struck. Captain Mike Gregory dropped a pass just inside our own half. Andy Farrell swooped on the loose ball and was tackled, fairly, by Paul Cullen. But the referee, Russell Smith, penalised Cull for using his knees when he didn't. Television replays proved that. Smith awarded a penalty 30 yards out, well within Frano Botica's range. But Jonathan Davies was so incensed that he went to speak to Smith, who marched us back another 10 yards because Jonathan wasn't the captain. Botica kicked the goal. They won 8–6 and we lost the title on points difference.

After the Sheffield game, a Warrington fan from Kent, called Barry Nash, rang the club to find out what the supporters had been chanting during the match. Cull said it was "Brian Johnson's Barmy Army". On hearing this Barry laughed and Cull asked him why. Barry said it made sense. He thought the fans had been singing "Brian Johnson's Ravioli" which didn't seem right. We might not have been "Brian Johnson's Ravioli" but were a tasty team.

Hooker John Thursfield, another Woolston Rovers lad, had his best season that year, playing in 32 of our 36 games. He had had to wait patiently behind Duane Mann and should have played a lot more games because he was a good player with a fast step and a great pair of hands. The ball hit the target every time.

Mark and Chris Rudd contest a high ball against Castleford in November 1993.

Mark looks to the official for support. (Both photos: Eddie Whitham).

I also scored my 100th try for Warrington: against Hull at Wilderspool on 6 February. Rob Myler, who was playing centre, made a great break and put me in the clear and I raced in from 40 yards. I was only the third Warrington-born player to reach three figures for the club – after Jim Tranter and Jim Challinor – and the first not to be called Jim. I said at the time: "To score 100 tries for one club is very special – in fact it is a dream come true. I think my best try was the one against Oldham which got us to Wembley in 1990. That was a special one but they all are – from one to 100."

But I was back on the transfer list again in June 1994. I must have rejected their contract offer. This time I was listed at £20,000 – up £5,000 from the previous summer – and I was still on the list when we played St Helens at Wilderspool in August. Once again I proved my worth with a first-half hat-trick, with all three coming from cross-field kicks, two from Greg Mackey and one from Jonathan Davies. I agreed a new contract soon after that.

I went one better at Wakefield in November when I scored four tries, 11 days before my 30th birthday. All four tries came in the second half after we had been losing 15–10 at half-time and helped us to win 32–26. I told the *Warrington Guardian* after the match: "There's life in the old dog yet!" Some of the Warrington fans at Belle Vue even sang "Fozzie for Britain" which was good to hear.

I played in all 40 of Warrington's games during the 1994–95 season and was our leading try-scorer with 24. Jonathan Davies and Iestyn Harris scored 18 each. The highlight of the season was our amazing run in the Regal Trophy. We beat Doncaster 44–14 at Wilderspool in the second round after trailing 14–12 at half-time and getting a roasting from Brian Johnson. We were on television in the third round against Salford at the Willows. The changing rooms at the Willows were under the stand and players soon learnt that if they didn't get in early and grab a peg at the top end they would be crouching down and banging their head all the time. Again, we were poor in the first half and behind 24–10 at half-time before a thrilling fightback took us to a 31–24 victory.

Next stop was a difficult trip to Cougar Park – Lawkholme Park – to play the Second Division leaders Keighley Cougars. To make matters worse, the drains had blocked up and sewerage had scattered across the pitch and mixed in with the mud. It took me two weeks to get rid of the smell. Again, we seemed to be heading for defeat until a last-gasp try and goal from Jonathan Davies let us sneak home 20–18. We were up against Widnes in the semi-finals and finally produced a convincing performance to win 30–4. I scored two tries, Iestyn Harris scored two tries and Jonathan Davies kicked four goals and two drop goals.

The final was against Wigan at the new Alfred McAlpine Stadium in Huddersfield in January 1995. It was the first time it had staged a major rugby league occasion and 19,636 fans turned up. I was a doubt all week with a rib cartilage injury. Right up to the very last minute I wasn't playing but then the club doctor, Dr Rothwell, said he could give me a pain-killing injection and I wouldn't feel my ribs until the next day, but then they would hurt like hell. It was a final and I asked if playing would make the injury worse. He said: "No. It won't make it any worse but you will be in an awful lot of pain tomorrow." I had the injection played in the final and scored two tries. I played the full 80 minutes and so I didn't let anybody down, but the following day I couldn't move and it felt like I had been kicked by a horse – several times. To add to the pain, Wigan had beaten us 40–10 with Inga the Winger scoring two tries and Frano Botica kicking eight goals.

Another Warrington lad, Andy Bennett, was one of the substitutes in the Regal Trophy final. He came on for hooker Tukere Barlow in the second half. I remember when he and another local lad, Lee Westwood, had just signed for Warrington as 17-year-olds and they came away on our end-of-season trip. I think it was to Ibiza. They were made our 'beer bitches'. If any of the first team squad wanted a beer they put their hand up for Andy or Lee to serve them and if the beer didn't arrive in two minutes they had to perform a forfeit – like being dragged along the beach. It was just a bit of fun and Andy asked me to be his best man a few years later. I also played alongside him as an amateur for Bank Quay Bulls and played for him when he became the Bulls coach. Andy developed the most bowed legs of any player I knew. He would not be able to stop a pig in an entry, that's for sure. He blamed it on all his years of playing rugby league. He recently had a replacement knee, so that one is straight, which makes the other leg look even worse!

I made my 300th start for Warrington at Widnes on Good Friday 1995 and celebrated with a try that Eddie Fuller, the *Warrington Guardian* photographer, later picked as his "try of the season". Against the run of play, Allan Bateman intercepted a stray ball and – like all wingers are supposed to do – I was backing up to take his pass and score. We went on to win 37–16. Eddie presented me with a framed photograph of the try at our annual awards presentation evening at the Lord Daresbury Hotel in May.

Warrington signed Andy Currier from Featherstone Rovers for the 1995–96 season to replace Allan Bateman who had joined Cronulla. Andy was a big, tall, gangly centre who had been a massive success at Widnes and that became a monkey on his back at Warrington. He also struggled with injuries and ended up going to South Wales on loan. Another signing that did not come off was that of 'Prince' Manoa Thompson, a winger from Fiji. We were all thinking "He has got to really love himself this guy to call himself 'Prince' Manoa Thompson" but it turned out that his father was a King back in Fiji and so Manoa was a Prince. But he was only an average player and did not enjoy the British winter. He didn't like the cold and the rain and the snow. He was a prince playing rugby, he just wasn't very good at it, and only lasted three months before returning home.

Dave King, an enormous Australian prop, did not last much longer than that. He had been a massive success at Huddersfield after joining them from London Crusaders, but did not make much of an impression at Warrington. The crowd got on his back so he returned to Huddersfield. We had a bit more luck with Mark Jones, the former Wales rugby union number 8, who we signed from Hull in July 1995. He was a man mountain and one of the funniest men I've ever met. He had had a problem with a stammer since he was at school, but when we went out and had a drink he was a great karaoke singer and never stuttered once. I have met him a few times in Cardiff at Challenge Cup finals and Millennium Magic Weekends and we always reminisce about the old days.

Top: Mark celebrates a try against Widnes at Wilderspool on Good Friday 1994. On the ground is Widnes winger Adrian Hadley. The try came from a Greg Mackey grubber kick to the corner.

Left: Mark waves to the crowd after scoring three first–half tries against St Helens at Wilderspool in August 1994. All three came from cross–field kicks, two from Greg Mackey and one from Jonathan Davies. Mark was on the transfer list at £20,000 at the time.

(Both photos: Eddie Fuller)

Left: Mark punching the air in 1994, after another try for Warrington.
(Photo: Eddie Fuller)

Bottom: Mark tackles Widnes winger Adrian Hadley in a Regal Trophy semi–final at Naughton Park in January 1995.
(Photo: Eddie Whitham).

Batley 22 Warrington 35
Sunday, 26 November 1995, Regal Trophy third round

I always liked playing on the big, wide grounds – which gave me more space – like Central Park, Knowsley Road and Headingley. Headingley, behind the scenes, was always more advanced than Wilderspool, Central Park, Naughton Park and Knowsley Road. It was all modern and I scored my first try for Great Britain there.

On the other hand, I remember going to Batley's Mount Pleasant ground once in the Regal Trophy in November 1995. They tell players about the famous slope and they think it can't be that bad, it can't be that bad. But I must say, it was. It was wet, miserable and raining and we played down the hill in the first half. The weather changed at half-time and in the second half we were playing up hill and into wind, rain and sleet. We won 35–22, but were glad when it was over. After that we beat Rochdale Hornets 38–20 in the fourth round – Andy Currier scored two tries – and were in the semi-finals with St Helens, Wigan and Leeds. We avoided Wigan, in the semi-final, but went to Knowsley Road instead.

St Helens 80 Warrington 0
Thursday, 4 January 1996, Regal Trophy semi-final

It was horrendous. Everything we tried, failed. Every bounce of the ball favoured St Helens. Simple moves that we had scored off many times in the previous two or three years, didn't work. We either dropped the ball or gave a forward pass and St Helens simply picked up the ball and went the length of the field to score. It was just one of those games – one of those games that I hope never to be involved in again. At the end of the game Brian Johnson, one of the best coaches I ever worked with, handed in his resignation. It wasn't Brian's fault. It was about players not being fully fit, about bad luck and about St Helens – and scrum-half Bobbie Goulding in particular – being red hot. But Brian decided to fall on his sword. Peter Higham, the Warrington chairman, said to him: "How can you resign when you don't have a contract?" Brian had been Warrington coach for eight years and never had a contract. It was a gentleman's agreement between Brian and Peter, such was the mutual respect and friendship between them. Paul Cullen doesn't like to be reminded of this match either: it was his first as Warrington captain.

At scrum-half that night, we had the former Wigan, Oldham and Castleford half-back Mike Ford, who had joined us from South Queensland Crushers. I was surprised when he became Ireland rugby union's defence coach in 2002 and then England rugby union's defence coach in 2006. When he was with us I thought he couldn't tackle a good Sunday dinner. He was a half-back who threw the ball around and had a good kicking game. He was fast on his feet and a quick thinker, but would admit that he wasn't the biggest hitter in rugby league. He was a great organiser, like Shaun Edwards, who became Wales rugby union defence coach, and his organisational skills help him as head coach at Bath.

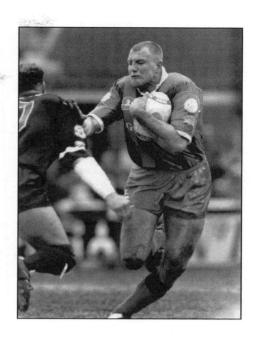
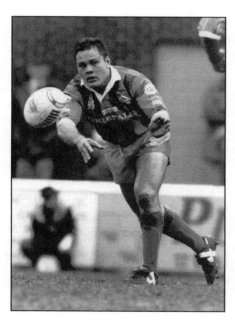

From top left, clockwise: Four team–mates from the 1994–95 season: full–back Lee Penny, prop Mark
'The Beast' Hilton, second row Gary Sanderson and hooker Tukere Barlow.
(All photos: courtesy Gary Slater)

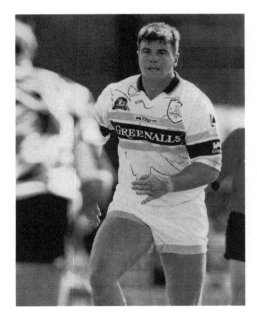

Four team–mates from the Centenary Season, 1995–96: hooker John Thursfield, loose–forward Mike Wainwright, prop Dave King and prop Mark Jones. (All photos: courtesy Gary Slater)

10. Super League

When the game went fully professional in 1995, Brian Johnson was given a list of 33 players on a Friday afternoon and told to get rid of a dozen or more. The rest of us would start full-time training on the Monday. You had to feel for Brian, it was a horrible job. He said: "Foz, I want you to go full-time." I was 30, but I agreed to do one year so that my sons, Chris and Dan, could see me play as they were growing up. But I found that because of the full-time training, the masseurs, doctors and dieticians, I became a better player and ended up doing five years of Super League. I enjoyed every minute of it.

So I became a full-time professional, but I also kept my full-time job. A new idea had been brought over from Australia that players trained at 6.30am before they had time to eat or drink. The idea was supposed to burn fat and build muscle better. I was in the gym at 6.30am, out at 7.30am, session done, and on the building site at eight. I then did a day's work as a builder on two local estates before the afternoon training session began at 3pm. I used to get changed in the van and have my flask and my breakfast in the van. I did that for 12 months until Roby Muller, the former Warrington forward, had a birthday party at Warrington Cricket Club. Peter Higham, the Warrington chairman, was there and he said: "You owe me £50,000." I said: "What?" He said: "You are supposed to be a full-time professional, but you've got a full-time job as well." I said: "It's done me no harm." He agreed and said: "I want you to take all the other players to work as well because they are playing rubbish."

Brian Johnson was replaced by the 'Dream Team' of coach John Dorahy and football executive Alex Murphy. We all knew what John Dorahy had done as a player with Hull KR and Halifax and he had just coached Wigan to the league and Challenge Cup double before being sacked. Alex Murphy was the king returning to his throne after the success of the 1970s. In some ways it was a strange relationship because we thought that Dorahy didn't really like Poms and Murph didn't really like Aussies. But they got on well and we played some good rugby to finish fifth in Super League I. Once again, I played in every game, as did a young Paul Sculthorpe.

Playing against Oldham Bears at Watersheddings that June I was knocked out and carried off on a stretcher. After that I started wearing a blue skullcap to give me some protection, but we didn't have the concussion tests they have now. If a player said he was fit he played the following week. In July we travelled to Derwent Park to play Workington Town. Appearing at stand-off for Town that day was a little-known Australian called Tony Smith. Workington were bottom of the table, Tony dropped the ball over the line when he should have scored and we won 49–4 – a record winning margin for an away game – and I scored two tries. Famously, Tony and his wife were living above a fish and chip shop in Workington and he later admitted: "Every morning I trudged to training and swore we'd never come back to this country." Thankfully, he changed his mind because he has gone on to make himself a legend in the minds of the Warrington public.

Warrington's squad for the 1996 Super League season. Left to right, back: Mateaki Mafi, Ian Knott, Mark Jones, Paul Sculthorpe, Mark Hilton, Toa Kohe–Love, Salesi Finau; middle: Phil Chadwick (trainer), Gary Chambers, Richard Henare, Jonathan Roper, Kelly Shelford, Mike Ford, Tony Rothwell (physio); front: John Hough, Iestyn Harris, John Dorahy (coach), Paul Cullen (captain), Alex Murphy (football executive), Lee Penny, Mark Forster. (Photo: Eddie Whitham).

I was only sin-binned once in my career and that was in July 1996 for fighting with the Bradford Bulls forward Sonny Nickle. It was a strange one because, believe it or not, Sonny and I were quite good friends at the time and still are. I tackled him on the left wing, the side of the Brian Bevan Stand at Wilderspool, and Sonny took an instant dislike to it. He played the ball and started throwing punches at me and so I started throwing punches at him. Then a scuffle broke out on the halfway line and then the other two wingers, Richard Henare and Glen Tomlinson, started fighting out of the blue. So there were three patches of fights going on. The referee, Stuart Cummings, didn't know which one to stop first. I suppose he could have sent six of us off. Sonny and I were sin-binned and Richard Henare was put on report and later banned for two matches. The other two fighters, whoever they were, got away with it. Needless to say, Sonny and I had a laugh about it in the bar afterwards, bought each other a pint and it was all forgotten about. What happens on the field, stays on the field.

The game was being covered by Sky Sports and during a race for the ball two Bradford players shoved me into the camera behind the try line. I put my elbows up to protect myself and cut both arms, but the cameraman came off even worse than me. The camera was smashed against his face and left a mark like a diver's mask.

Mark Hilton takes on the Paris St Germain forwards, with Mark Forster in support, at Wilderspool in April 1996.

Mark in action against Leeds at Wilderspool in June 1996. (Both photos: Eddie Whitham)

Mark boots the ball up field against Wigan at Wilderspool in June 1996.

Mark stops a Castleford player in a 'ball and all' tackle in August 1996.
(Both photos: Eddie Whitham)

Friends reunited: Mark tackled by Oldham's former Warrington half–back Martin Crompton at Wilderspool in August 1996. Martin had had his hair bleached blond to raise money for charity. He looked different, but it was for a good cause. (Photo: Eddie Whitham)

Warrington players celebrate a try at Wilderspool in 1997. Left to right: Salesi Finau, Mike Wainwright in his skullcap, Tony Tatupu, Willie Swann, a young Lee Briers, Paul Sculthorpe and veteran Mark Forster. (Photo: Eddie Fuller)

A few days later I was sent a bill for £3,200 from Sky for damage to the camera. I took it straight to the club and they told me that Sky wouldn't send me a bill like that. It was a wind-up. But it was a very clever wind-up – the bill even had the Sky Sports logo on it – and I fell for it hook, line and sinker. I still don't know who was responsible.

Before the start of the 1997 season, John Dorahy took us to an Army boot camp near Preston. John thought it would be great to get us all away. The instructors flogged us morning, noon and night. We weren't allowed to walk anywhere. If we went to the toilet we had to run. If we went to be sick, we had to run.

One night we were told we would be "milling" in the morning. "Milling" is a form of boxing, using massive, 20 pounds-plus gloves. There is no ducking, no weaving and no fancy footwork. Just taking hits and dishing them out. I said to Mateaki Mafi, a winger who had joined us from Tongan rugby union, that I was no good at boxing. He said he wasn't either and so we agreed that we would fight each other and just get through the three, three-minute rounds because just carrying the gloves was going to be hard enough. We got in the ring and all the other players started laughing because it was two wingers against each other. Mateaki had a gold tooth and it was shining. Then he started to knock me all around the ring. I said to him: "I thought you had never boxed before." He said: "I have never boxed before – in Preston, but I am a junior champion." He battered me all the way around the ring, but the ring was a ring of players and they kept pushing me back in the middle. I told him later: "You lied to me." He said he thought I had been lying to him.

A few years ago I was working in Cardiff and walking down the main street, minding my own business, when I felt a thud on my back and found myself in a headlock. I said: "Mate, I don't know who you are and I've done nothing wrong. Can you please get off?" A voice said: "You don't know who it is, do you Foz? I will give you a clue. I used to have a gold tooth." I said "Mateaki Mafi" and he let me go. It turned out he was working as a door supervisor at one of the shops.

On the last night in Preston, the two instructors took us out for a drink. They looked just like Phil and Grant Mitchell from *East Enders*. They were horrible, with big scars on the backs of their heads like they had had their brains taken out. They took us out drinking until about five in the morning. It was great. We were all bladdered and fell into bed at different times, from four o'clock to half past five. Gary Chambers was the last one to get to bed. Little did we know, but at 6.30am all the doors were thrown back off their hinges and the Mitchell brothers came in, dragged us all out of bed and took us on a massive hike. We were carrying trees around and all sorts of stuff. Gary Chambers made about 30 yards before he was violently sick and they made him run to the front. They had heard that we had been calling them the Mitchell brothers and they flogged us.

Also that night we had gone to a kebab shop in Preston and some locals came in and pushed to the front of the queue. Then the Preston lads started on us and it turned into a mass brawl. The shop was only 8 feet by 5 feet and Paul Sculthorpe took a couple of them out.

John Dorahy didn't last long as coach after the boot camp. His last act was to book the hotels for the World Club Challenge games in Australia and New Zealand and he got that wrong too. Our hotel was in the student quarters in Darling Harbour – the students had gone home for the summer – but there was nowhere to train or socialise. It was just basic student accommodation. When we bumped into the St Helens players or the Wigan players they were all in the trendy area, Coogee Bay, having a great time.

Another Australian, Darryl van de Velde, was our next coach and his first signing was a young kid from St Helens called Lee Briers. He came with a bit of baggage, which was understandable, because he had been dropped by St Helens for the Challenge Cup Final after playing in the earlier rounds. He wanted to prove St Helens wrong. As a senior player, I was already keeping an eye on young lads like Iestyn Harris, Jonathan Roper and Paul Sculthorpe and Darryl said: "Here's another one for you." Once Lee calmed down a bit we could see he was going to be a legend. He had the pace, the footwork, the brain and the kicking game. All the lads nicknamed him 'Kes' after the boy in the Ken Loach film. He was a right scruff. He would come to training in odd socks and ripped gear and he's still exactly the same.

Lee made his debut at St Helens, two days after signing for us, and we were hammered 60–16. I scored two tries that afternoon, including my 150th for Warrington, but personal milestones don't really mean very much when the team suffers a defeat like that.

Iestyn Harris was a brilliant young player but, for some reason, he would leave his training kit in his car for weeks on end and keep on using it and reusing it. His mum and dad reckoned he only emptied his car of training kit when there was nothing new left in the cupboard. The smell that came out of his car when he opened the boot was dreadful. Players would leg it as soon as he went to open it.

Scully had the skills, the dedication and a huge desire to win. He could play someone at shove ha'penny and have to win. He had that winning mentality and it was clear, from an early age, that he would be a club captain, play for Great Britain and go on to do great things in the game. Iestyn Harris and Paul Sculthorpe – two lads from Oldham – saved Warrington rugby league club but, unfortunately, they had to be sold to do so. Iestyn joined Leeds for £350,000 in April 1997 while Scully moved to St Helens for £370,000 that December. Talent like that cannot be easily replaced.

We also signed a huge Tongan centre called Salesi Finau. Our groundsman and kitman Ockher moaned like crazy because he had to get XXX large shorts for Salesi and XXX small shorts for Lee. Lee could fit in one leg of Salesi's shorts and have room to turn around. Gaynor and I went to Salesi's wedding at the Fir Grove Hotel in Warrington and I was the only white man there. I knew all the Pacific Islanders, we had a few beers and I told them I was a ghost.

Two more new signings were centre Toa Kohe-Love, a Junior Kiwi from Wellington, and scrum-half Willie Swann, a Western Samoan from Auckland Warriors. They both lived in Great Sankey and I was always doing jobs on my house in Penketh. The islanders always thought they could do any job and so I said to them: "I bet you can't climb trees." They

93

said they could and so I asked them to climb this massive silver birch in my back garden and cut some off the top.

Time flew by after that and we forgot about training and arrived two hours late. Darryl van de Velde was not amused. He said: "Why have three of you come in the same car, late for training and covered in scratches and mud? What have you been up to?" Toa and Willie grassed me up straight away. "Foz has had us cutting a tree down," they said together. "Is this true?" asked Darryl. I said it was and I copped the fine for all three of us.

Nigel Vagana, who had been in the Western Samoa squad for the 1995 Centenary World Cup when he was aged only 20, was Warrington's big signing for the 1997 season. Apparently when Warrington asked Auckland Warriors about signing him they said we could have Nigel if we took Tony Tatupu, a second-row forward, as well because he was on so much money. Nigel had a great season, scoring 22 tries in 30 matches, and so Auckland wanted him back. Warrington said they could have Nigel back if they took Tony back as well because he was on so much money and hadn't had the best of seasons – so he went back the same way he arrived.

I remember one match when Alex Murphy was our football executive and was in the dug-out and Tony was having a nightmare. I was on the left wing and all I could hear was Murphy shouting "rubbish" and "useless" and things like that. It was echoing around the stadium. Murph shouted to me: "Foz, get over there and tell him that if he doesn't buck his ideas up he will be on the next plane home." I pretended not to hear and so Murph shouted again: "Foz, get over here." Again, I pretended not to hear, but when he shouted me for a third time I thought I'd better go over. It was the same message: "Tell him that if he doesn't buck his ideas up he will be on the next plane home."

I ran over to the middle of the field where Taps was and said: "Taps, Murph said you're playing fantastic, keep it up." Taps turned his game around completely after that, scored a try and we ended up winning the game.

Auckland Warriors prop Dallas Mead was another big signing for the 1997 season, but I thought that he wasn't a very good trainer. We played Salford in a pre-season warm-up match that January and he injured his knee ligaments or his ankle ligaments and the first thing he did was tidy his hair and that didn't go down very well with the fans. He thought his pre-season training was bouncing up and down on a one metre round trampoline to get himself fit. Phil Chadwick, our sprint trainer, wasn't having that. So Chaddy had him, in the middle of Victoria Park, bouncing on it – up and down – for an hour and a half to try to get him fit. Dallas only played two games for us. He became a professional wrestler when he had retired from playing rugby which just proves how fake wrestling can be.

I thought that Chaddy was as mad as a box of frogs. He used to train every day of the year, even Christmas Day. There were some hills in Bewsey and they used to call them "Chaddy's Hills" because he was always running up and down them. He arrived for training at Victoria Park once in the winter era wearing trainers and shorts but no socks and no top. We all said he was mad because he must be freezing. He said: "It's you lot who are mad. When I finish training I've got a lovely warm tracksuit, a lovely hoodie and dry socks waiting in my car. You will be sitting in wet, damp clothes on the way home." So, the following session, we all trained in just boots and shorts.

He always said: "If it was easy this training pitch would be full and people would be queuing around the block to play for Warrington. It's not easy." We could never say to Chaddy "You can't do that, you can't do 50 press-ups" because he would do double that number and then we would have to do double that number as well. He was one of the fittest guys around and it was all self-taught. He used to say things like: "I've had a pint of cabbage water before I trained today. Boiled the cabbage, threw the cabbage away and drank the water because that is where all the vitamins are." After that we all started drinking cabbage water.

Years later I did a couple of sessions with him in a boxing ring when I was playing for Bank Quay Bulls as an amateur. He said "Foz, it must be 20 years since we were training together" and he gave me a big hug. It was supposed to be a 45 seconds session, but he could see I was flagging a bit and so he kept me in the ring and battered me for three and a half minutes. All the Bank Quay lads said "I'm not going in there with him if he does that to you Foz."

He got the sack from Warrington after the World Club Challenge match against Cronulla at Wilderspool in June 1997 when a male streaker ran across the pitch. Chaddy was the conditioner and water carrier that day and offered the streaker a drink of water. The streaker took the water bottle, had a drink and then carried on running. Chaddy was dragged in front of the board and they got rid of him for helping the streaker.

I was lucky enough to share a room with Nigel Vagana for the World Club Challenge matches in Australia in July 1997 and he, basically, stopped out every night and partied and so I had the room to myself, which was really good. Nigel would get in at 7am, have a shower and be on the training field for 8am. Two days before we were due to leave Darryl van de Velde was going out for his morning paper at about 7.30am and saw Nigel coming back with all his party gear on. Darryl read the riot act to him, but Nigel said he had been doing that for two weeks and Darryl hadn't noticed.

While we were there Darryl, Paul Sculthorpe, Lee Briers and myself did some commentary work for Fox TV on the other games. Lee and Darryl did the first game and Scully and I did the second. We only spoke about five sentences and we were paid $500 each. Darryl came out and said he could not believe that Lee – who was still very shy – was on more money than Michael Jackson. He said Lee had answered two questions with yes and no and walked away with $500 in his pocket so he was on $250 per word!

We lost to Penrith Panthers and Cronulla Sharks and then we went over to New Zealand and had to play the Auckland Warriors. There were six inches of water on the pitch in Auckland and it was a freezing cold night. Straight from a scrum I scooted in from my wing and this time it wasn't a loose-forward waiting for me: it was big Joe Vagana. He hit me on the left-hand side so hard that when I landed on my right-hand side I hurt my bicep tendons and my shoulder tendons; and he left me in a pool of water. It was a fair shot, there was no malice in it; it was just the ferocity of the challenge.

Remembering Princess Dianna with a minute's silence before the game against Oldham
at Boundary Park in August 1997.

Left: Mark scored against Bradford Bulls in
his 400th appearance for Warrington in
June 1998.

(Both photos: Eddie Whitham)

Left: Mark tackling Bradford's Stuart Spruce on his 400th appearance for Warrington in June 1998.

Below: Mark scoring against Huddersfield in September 1998 during the match to celebrate 100 years of rugby league at Wilderspool

(Both photos: Eddie Whitham)

They left me in the pool of water and carried on playing and I ended up with hypothermia. Three little St John Ambulance women – all aged at least 60 – looked after me and gave me a cup of tea. By the time I thawed out in the dressing room all the lads came in after the match and they were freezing as well. They said: "We lost anyway. You were probably in the best place."

In August we travelled to Bayonne, in the south of France, to play Paris St Germain, knowing that we had to win to avoid relegation. We took two planes and three coaches to get there. I scored two tries and we won 17–10, so Darryl van de Velde gave us two days off. However, it took us two days to get home and so we were straight back into training.

Warrington's Supporters' Club named me as their player of the year for 1997. It was my 16th season in the first team and the first time I had won the award and so I think I had deserved it. I had played in 28 matches and scored 12 tries in a struggling team. Darryl had also asked me to step up my work rate by coming inside and doing some runs for the props and I was happy to do that. I was also named the *Warrington Guardian* Sports Personality of the Year, another accolade I was proud to receive.

I was made up in 1998 when Warrington signed the New Zealand loose-forward Brendon Tuuta – "the baby-faced assassin" – and even more pleased when we signed "T" – Tawera Nikau – from Melbourne Storm two years later. They were both loose-forwards who had smashed me at the backs of scrums when I did the famous Warrington first-tackle scoot. When Tawera arrived we changed the play a little bit. He would pick the ball up from the base of the scrum – at that time that was allowed – and take the first drive and I would take the second drive. That broke the pattern up a little bit.

Also in 1998 we signed a young prop called Danny Nutley, who was so keen he wanted to play the full 80 minutes every week. Danny came to Ireland international squad training with me a few times and, of course, met up with those two jokers Barrie McDermott and Terry O'Connor who were busy polishing up their double act ready for a career on Sky Sports. They said: "You are mad Danny. Why do you want to play the full 80 minutes? You get the same money if you play 20 minutes in the first half and 20 minutes in the second."

Another new signing was Steve McCurrie, known as 'Spud', who was a great character. He made his debut for Widnes in 1990 when he was just 16 and was already being tipped to be a Great Britain hooker. When he came to Warrington, after a spell in rugby union with Bedford, we all knew him. He slotted straight into the team in the second row and scored some important tries. These days he is a driving instructor and he was my coach at Bank Quay Bulls when Chris, Dan and I all played there. He taught a few of the Bank Quay players how to drive and I asked them what it was like being taught by him. "It's great," they told me. "We go to the drive through at McDonald's and we go to the bookies!"

Warrington 28 Bradford Bulls 10
Sunday, 7 June 1998, JJB Super League
This was my 400th game for Warrington and it was a day when everything went right. Danny Farrar, our hooker and captain, asked me to lead the team out and, on the pitch, I

was presented with a pair of golden boots from our kit sponsors New Balance. At the time there were only two people in the country with these golden boots, me and the former Manchester United captain Bryan Robson. Chants of "Fozzie, Fozzie" echoed around the stadium. Before the match Darryl told me I would score two tries – and I did. The second, in particular, was a beauty. In the build-up to the match we had been watching video clips of Bradford and I saw that my opposite number, Tevita Vaikona, had been hanging back in defence. But, for once, he came up and Danny spotted it. He nodded to me that the move was on and sent a pin-point accurate kick to the corner. I raced in and touched down, but Stevo still never named me as the man-of-the-match. Danny was a great leader and tremendous signing from Penrith Panthers. He was coming towards the end of his career and didn't do much training at the start of the week, but by the weekend he was always fit and raring to go. He was a genuine guy and liked to celebrate good victories. He was also very generous after this match. He told the press: "I was pleased for Fozzie on his 400th appearance. That's a great effort. He's a legend isn't he?"

Salford 14 Warrington 25
Sunday, 5 July 1998, JJB Super League
Legend or not I was brought back down to earth at the Willows the following month. I scored a try and then covered up to protect myself because Gary Broadbent, the Salford full-back, was heading towards me. Unfortunately I caught him under the chin with my elbow and knocked him out. I wasn't sent off and I wasn't put on report but the RFL took a look at the video and I was dragged to Red Hall. David Campbell, the former referee from St Helens, was on the disciplinary panel. He gave me a three-game ban and a £150 fine and said: "By the way, will you look after my son Chris because he's just signed for Warrington." I said: "Of course I will." After that, I appealed against the three matches and had it reduced to two. But it was still disappointing because I had played in Warrington's last 41 matches, going back to March the previous year. I missed the "on the road" game against Castleford at Cardiff Arms Park and the home match against London Broncos; Warrington lost them both.

After my sons Chris and Dan started playing junior rugby we found it hard to get particular sports gear for them and we spoke to parents at Rylands ARLFC and they were struggling to find the right gear too. Head guards, shoulder pads, that sort of thing. So Gaynor and I thought we would open a shop and so Fozzies Sportswear was born in Latchford village in November 1998. It was a big success for four years.

The actor Steve Arnold, who played Ashley Peacock on *Coronation Street*, was one of the lads I knocked around with at the time and he opened the shop for me. *Coronation Street* had just killed off the character Des Barnes, played by Philip Middlemiss, and so the cast had a great big party. Steve was there all night, the night before we opened the shop, and so he was quite hungover. Plus there were about 150 kids all calling him Ashley. Another friend of ours was going round with champagne and kept shouting: "Do you want some champagne Ashley?" He said: "Will you stop calling me Ashley?" But he was great and we had Wolfie there, the Warrington Wolves mascot, and brought Latchford village to a standstill, stopping the traffic going through it.

It was wonderful when we won on a Sunday and the fans came in the following week, but if we lost I used to take Mondays off. The kids were delighted to be sold a Warrington top or a pair of boots by a Warrington player. However, after three years or so JJB Sports opened a store down the road and that didn't help. All the parents wanted to come to my shop for the cheaper prices, but the kids wanted to go to JJB for the plastic bag they could carry their stuff around in. So that was the end of Fozzies Sportswear.

I wore a pair of bright yellow boots from Fozzies Sportswear for the Chris Rudd and Gary Chambers testimonial match at Wilderspool in November 1998. Chris and Gary were two lads from the Kells amateur club in Cumbria who had made their careers and their homes in Warrington. Both played well over 100 games for the first team. Their testimonial match pitted a Warrington XIII against a Cumbrian XIII and for once, even though I was nearly 34, I wasn't the oldest player in the Warrington team because three legends had come out of retirement for the afternoon – scrum-half Andy Gregory aged 37, second row Bob Eccles – 41 and prop Kevin Tamati – 44.

Another former Warrington prop, Tony Humphries, got the ball rolling with a high tackle on the club doctor, Graham Scott, who was foolishly playing in the second row for Cumbria. After that Warrington built up a 26–0 lead with tries from Phil Chadwick, our former fitness coach who was playing at full-back, Bob Eccles, stand-off Andy Green, Andy Gregory, winger Richard Henare and former Academy player Andy James. Cumbria hit back with tries from the former Swinton professional Billy Lomax and left winger Graham Lewthwaite to make the half-time score 26–10.

The second half descended into chaos after Rudd and Chambers, who were both playing for Cumbria, decided that the game should be played with a blow-up sheep instead of a ball. They also both played in wellies for the occasion – to make them feel at home. Thankfully, the blow-up sheep soon burst and so we could get back to playing with a proper ball and run in more tries. The match finished with a 60–40 victory for Warrington and the final Cumbrian try came from that well-known son of Cumberland, Mateaki Mafi.

The referee was Bob Connolly and he actually blew the final whistle eight minutes early, saying: "I wanted to save the supporters from further punishment." I had played in the second row and was named man-of-the-match by the *Warrington Guardian* with a score of 10 out of 10. The *Warrington Guardian* was my sponsor at the time, but I am sure that had nothing to do with the decision. The Touchdown Club was packed afterwards, everyone had a good afternoon and we raised some money for two top lads. I did a sportsman's dinners at Kells once and, believe it or not, they asked me back the following year.

11. The End

Lord Hoyle, who used to be plain old Doug Hoyle, the Labour MP for Warrington North, became the chairman of Warrington Wolves in 1999 and was introduced to the players in the changing room before a match. We all sat in order, starting on the left with Lee Penny the full-back and then me. So Doug walked in and was introduced to Lee. "Hello Lee, pleased to meet you," that sort of thing. Now, at the time, there was a bin strike on in Warrington, so when it was my turn I just said: "I am not happy Doug." He asked me why and I said: "Am I going to get my bins emptied this week?" The dressing room cracked up and, to be fair, Doug said: "Foz, there is only you would ask me that. I am chairman of the club." I said: "My bins are overflowing." Anyway, it broke the ice and made him feel welcome. Doug told me later that he had been a little bit worried about going into the dressing room, but that made him one of the lads. It also relaxed the players and we went on to win the match comfortably. I asked Darryl van de Velde for a pay rise after that and he said: "You're not having one and you won't make it as a comedian either."

Warrington also made two big signings: Peter Deakin and Alan Hunte. Peter had worked wonders with his marketing skills at Bradford Bulls and Saracens rugby union club and arrived as chief executive on a three-year contract. Alan, the former St Helens and Great Britain centre, came on a free transfer from Hull Sharks, as Hull FC were known at the time. Alan was seriously quick, but I always say that I was faster than him and here is why. At St Helens, Barrie Ledger said that he was faster than Alan Hunte and I beat Barrie Ledger in the race to be the fastest man in rugby league in 1986. So that will do me, although Alan may not agree. Alan and I both scored hat-tricks against Featherstone Rovers in the fourth round of the Challenge Cup. I was voted the Silk Cut man-of-the-match by the press and received a medal and £200. We beat Halifax in the next round before losing at Bradford in the quarter-finals. We only finished seventh in the JJB Sports Super League, but there was a feeling that we were making progress.

I broke my arm playing for Ireland against Scotland in Dublin in October 1999. More of that later. But, at the time, I did not realise that I had broken it and so just carried on playing, like rugby league players do. I even scored a try. I had a plate fitted in the arm when I got back to England. I was out for three months, but fit for the start of the 2000 season, Super League V. I made my comeback at Hunslet in the fourth round of the Challenge Cup in February and scored a try. But just as I was returning to action my son Chris broke his left arm playing for Rylands Sharks under–12s. Like me, he did not realise he had broken it, carried on playing and kicked a goal. That must say something about the Forsters!

The 2000 season was going to be a big one because Warrington had signed three legends of the game in Allan Langer, Tawera Nikau and Andrew Gee. Another Woolston Rovers lad, Mike Wainwright, had been holding his own as loose-forward, but as soon as they signed Nikau that was it. Mike's contract offer was withdrawn and he joined Salford.

Sometimes, to be honest, Mike would have played better than "T" but that didn't matter. "T" was the big name.

I had grown up watching Alfie Langer. He was always on the Kangaroo tours and always the main man. He had done everything, maybe done everything twice, but he was still down to earth. He still comes over once or twice a year to this day and sometimes stops with friends down the road from me. He knocks on the front door when he is on his way to the Rope and Anchor pub and asks if I am going out as if we are two 10-year-olds going out to play.

Nikau and Langer were both absolute legends of the game, but were also arch rivals because one was a Kiwi and one was a Kangaroo, although they became great friends at Warrington. Tragically, Tawera came off his motorbike back home in New Zealand in 2003 and lost his right leg. So what did Alfie send him to cheer him up? A pair of socks. He said they would last him for two days instead of one. There is probably only Alfie Langer who could get away with that.

Alfie came over from Brisbane Broncos with the former Queensland prop Andrew Gee. Gee Gee, as he was known, was a big unit and always wanted to play the full 80 minutes. He was an absolute workhorse. He gave 110 per cent in every game and training session. His body at the end of a game was so battered and bruised that we wondered how he could play the next week never mind the next training session. But he very rarely missed a training session and was a top guy off the field as well.

With Nikau, Langer and Gee Gee in the team we beat York 84–1 at Wilderspool in the next round of the Challenge Cup with stand-off Lee Briers scoring a club record 40 points from three tries and 14 goals. He loved playing with Alfie. In the quarter-finals we went to Salford and seemed to be heading out of the competition when we trailed 20–18 in the fifth minute of injury time. But then Toa Kohe-Love sent Alan Hunte over, in front of the BBC cameras, and we won 22–20.

In the semi-finals we played Bradford Bulls at Headingley in March. Four of us were in our 30s. I was 35, Langer and Nikau were 33 and Danny Farrar was 31 while Alan Hunte and Andrew Gee were both 29. This was our one and only chance to get to the final as a group. In the build-up to the match the *Daily Express* even ran a story about me picking up my pension – and it was sort of true. When I was 25 or 26 I had started paying into a professional sportsman's pension and it had matured the previous November when I was 35, although I hadn't started claiming it because I was still playing. The headline said: "Warrington winger picks up his pension". Thanks a lot! We gave the semi-final our best shot and Steve McCurrie scored two tries, but Bradford were too good for us in the end and won 44–20. They went on to lift the cup as well, beating Leeds Rhinos in the final at Murrayfield. It would have been amazing for Alfie and I and the rest to play there.

The following month we went to Wakefield for a game that Dean Busby, a second-row forward signed from St Helens, will never forget – no matter how hard he tries. We had scored five tries – through me, Alan Hunte, Danny Nutley, Allan Langer and Steve McCurrie – and were leading 24–22 with only seconds left. Wakefield were awarded a penalty and a chance to salvage an undeserved draw, but Steve McNamara's kicked drifted harmlessly across the face of goal and towards Dean. All he had to do was catch it and we had won the match. But he didn't. He dropped it and Willie Poching followed up to score a try and win the match for Wakefield. Darryl van der Velde was livid. He said: "All they had to do was catch the ball. Six-year-old kids are taught to catch the ball." Ouch!

Our next match was against Leeds at Wilderspool and disaster, personal disaster anyway, struck again. Leroy Rivett, the Leeds winger, was going in for a try and I moved in to tackle him, but he slipped, landed on my forearm and broke my arm again through the plate. That was the last thing I needed at the age of 35. I was back in hospital again the following day and had the plate taken out. Now I've got a bent arm which will have to be operated on again when I finally retire from the amateur game. I was out of action for four months while it healed, but back in the team for the last month of the season. I even scored a try – my 191st for Warrington – at Wakefield in September. I am proud of all my tries and this one is no exception. Lee Briers put in a high kick and the ball was dropped by the Wakefield winger, a young lad named Ben Westwood – I wonder what happened to him – and I nipped in to score. We won 26–18.

The following Sunday was our last game of the season, at home to Salford, and – although I didn't know it at the time – my last game for Warrington. It was also Danny Farrar's last game for Warrington, we all knew that, and he was given a rousing send-off after his three years at Wilderspool. Steve McCurrie scored two tries, Alan Hunte scored two tries, Alfie Langer kicked four goals, we won 38–10 and everyone went home happy – although not straight away.

Another Australian, the stand-off Chris O'Sullivan, had brought the idea of a 'Mad Monday' with him when he joined us from Canberra Raiders in 1990. All the players would meet at Wilderspool on the Monday after the end of the season, have the last video session, hand out certain awards and then drink the stadium dry. When Alfie and Gee Gee arrived in 2000 they took 'Mad Monday' to a whole new level. After beating Salford we went to the Village Hotel as normal. Alfie and Gee Gee then said to their wives: "We will see you on Wednesday." 'Mad Monday' now lasted for three days and no one was allowed to go home. They booked themselves into the Village Hotel for three nights, but didn't have any spare clothes with them.

After two days of drinking they decided to buy some more clothes and went to the St Rocco's charity shop in Stockton Heath. They bought the silliest outfits they could find. One bought Mr Blobby slippers, another bought a blouse and they left the labels on. They following year everyone did it. St Rocco's used to look forward to it.

I had always wanted to be a one-club man. I was a Warrington lad and a proud Warringtonian. I was lucky enough to be awarded a second testimonial season at Warrington and Darryl van de Velde said he was going to offer me a new contract for 12 months for 2001, but he couldn't give me any extra money. I said that was fine. We shook hands and agreed on it and I went away a happy lad. That was on Monday, 25 September.

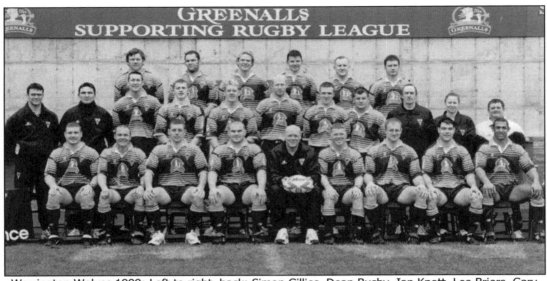

Warrington Wolves 1999: Left to right, back: Simon Gillies, Dean Busby, Ian Knott, Lee Briers, Gary Chambers, Dean Hanger; middle: Paul Darbyshire, Paul Cullen, Mike Wainwright, Jamie Stenhouse, Lee Penny, Jason Roach, Will Cowell, Danny Nutley, Terry Gilogley (training manager), physio Stephanie Rea, Dr Graham Scott; front: Jonathan Roper, Scott Wilson, Mark Forster, Steve McCurrie, coach Darryl van de Velde, Danny Farrar, Mark Hilton, Toa Kohe-Love, Alan Hunte.
(Photo: Eddie Fuller)

Mark in action against Gateshead Thunder at Wilderspool in April 1999.

(Photo: Eddie Whitham)

Back to front: Warrington's squad for the 2000 season. Left to right, back: Andrew Gee, Steve Blakeley, Gary Chambers, Dean Busby, Ian Knott, Ian Sibbit; middle: Paul Darbyshire, David Highton, Danny Nutley, Mark Forster, Danny Farrar and Jerome Guisset; front: Alan Hunte, Neil Parsley, Lee Briers, Tawera Nikau, Darryl van de Velde (coach), Allan Langer, Steve McCurrie, Lee Penny, Toa Kohe-Love, Jonathan Roper. (Photo: Eddie Whitham)

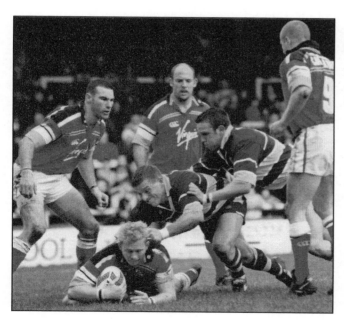

Mark tackles London Broncos' Tulsen Tollett in March 2000 on one of his last appearances for Warrington.

(Both photos: Eddie Whitham)

On the Friday morning I did a presentation at the Alderman Bolton Community Primary School in Warrington from 9am until 9.15am and was in the office at Wilderspool by 20 past. Darryl never once stopped writing or looked me in the eye, but said he had changed his mind. He said he could get three players – Chris Campbell, Jamie Stenhouse and Will Cowell – for the money I was on. I don't know how he did it because I was only on a guaranteed £21,000 a year. They must have got £7,000 a year each for being supposed Super League players. I had a few words with him and stormed out. The office staff couldn't believe it and to this day he hasn't really explained why he changed his mind. None of this came out at the time though. It was only when I appeared on *Super League Superstars* on Sky Sports in 2013 that a lot of Warrington fans found out the truth. When Darryl comes over now to visit Warrington, my wife Gaynor won't speak to him although I am sure he thought he was doing his best for the club. But between them Chris Campbell – 7 games, Jamie Stenhouse – 12 and Will Cowell – 6, started just 25 games for Warrington. I was suspended for almost that many.

That wasn't the end of the story. Kevin Campion, the Brisbane Broncos loose-forward, was supposed to be joining Warrington for 2001, but changed his mind after finding out how I had been treated and signed for New Zealand Warriors instead. Kevin came over to play for Ireland in the 2000 Rugby League World Cup with fellow Australians Luke Ricketson and Danny Williams. I had only just been introduced to Kevin and he said: "Foz, what's happened to you?" We sat down and had a game of cards and a few beers and I told him the story. He said: "There is no way I am signing for Warrington. If they can do that to you after 20 years, what are they going to do to me after 20 months?" I told him to go down to the club and meet the office staff, the players and the fans and he would love them all. Kevin did just that on his day off. He said I was absolutely right about the office staff, the players and the fans and the set-up, but that he didn't warm to Darryl van de Velde and wouldn't be signing. A story came out in the press that he had changed his mind because of the terrible English weather, but that wasn't the case. Darryl signed another Brisbane Broncos player, Kevin Walters, instead.

Everybody I speak to about Darryl van de Velde says the same thing, Warrington players, Castleford players and Huddersfield players, everywhere he has been. If someone was in his first team and playing well, he was your best friend, the best thing since sliced bread. If you were playing badly or injured or suspended you were out of the loop. He could walk past in a metre wide corridor and completely ignore you. He could blank you in a telephone box. Dean Sampson, the Castleford prop, told me it was exactly the same there. But there are also stories that, at Warrington, when the club was having financial problems, he paid the players' wages himself for one or two months and never got paid himself.

At the time I was one of the few players who had my own house and garden in Warrington and so the club decided that the end-of-season barbecue or pre-season barbecue would be at my house and the club would foot the bill. I would always burn the first half-dozen burgers and the first half-dozen sausages and smoke would go everywhere.

Darryl would say: "You Poms can't do a barbecue. Let me take over and show you how it's done." He would push me out of the way and take over. That suited me down to the ground because I was then free to socialise and have a drink. Darryl fell for it every time.

One year we had a magician and the three- and four-year-olds could tell how he was doing the tricks, but our prop Warren Stevens was amazed. "How's he doing that?" he asked. He was a lovely lad, a very skilful player who could hold his own against the best, and never took a backward step, but I thought he wasn't the brightest bulb in the shop.

Mark Hilton – 'The Beast' – was another prop who was totally dedicated. He was in the dressing room and changed before most players had even arrived at the ground. I remember playing a match with him one hot, summer's day – when we were all struggling to breathe – and, at half-time, he told the club doctor, Dr Graham Scott, to take all his teeth out. They were stopping him from breathing properly. Dr Scott said they would talk about it after the match, by which time, thankfully, it had all been forgotten. But 'The Beast' was not a typical prop. He became a maths teacher at Great Sankey High School when he retired from playing in 2006. Not many props do that.

My second testimonial year went ahead as planned and my testimonial match was on Wednesday 14 February 2001, St Valentine's Day, against Wigan at Wilderspool. It was chucking it down. I thought I had an agreement with Warrington that any first team squad players who had not played a full 80 minutes the previous Sunday could play for me. But the day before the match I was told I could not have anyone from the first team squad and so I had to get a load of amateurs to play for me instead. But that wasn't the only difficulty on the night. My treasurer was my sister-in-law, Allison Lyons, and she was wrongly told by a Warrington representative that there was an outstanding bill owed to the club by Fozzies Sportswear. She was told that if she did not pay the bill there and then from the money coming in at the turnstiles the floodlights would be switched off at half-time. She didn't know what to do and got very upset. She said the money coming across the turnstiles had nothing to do with Fozzies Sportswear and didn't belong to Mark Forster. It belonged to the testimonial committee until the end of the testimonial year and she refused to pay. She told the man that the club would look ridiculous if they switched the lights off at half-time and, thankfully, common sense prevailed.

I walked out on the pitch for the last time as a player with my three children, Chris, Dan and Beckie by my side. They were wearing specially-made jerseys with the number five and "My Dad" on the back. Wigan put a strong side out, which was great of them, and they were too good for us. Phil Jones, the Wigan stand-off, scored a hat-trick of tries in the first half and kicked six goals; they won 48–12. Eric Andrews and hooker Mark Smith grabbed two tries each; second-row Simon Haughton and centre Martin Aspinwall also scored. Hooker Mark Gleeson, full-back Dave Alstead and I were the most experienced players in the Warrington team. I played at centre. John Hill, George Kay and Mark Gleeson scored our tries and Dave Alstead converted all three, including a superb effort from the touchline. With about five minutes left, a young Sean O'Loughlin – who was only 18 at the time – caught me on the nose and broke it and blood started pouring out.

Mark received a presentation at Warrington Town Hall in 2001 to mark his 20 years as a Warrington player. Also pictured from left: Tony Barrow, Ken Kelly, Alex Murphy and Doug Hoyle.

(Photo: courtesy Forster family)

The referee, Steve Ganson, said: "Who's done that?" I said: "It's your job to watch, isn't it?" My nose was cleaned up, but started bleeding again. Ganson said: "I can't send you to the blood bin in your own testimonial game. Shall I blow up five minutes early?" I agreed and that was that, my last appearance in a Warrington shirt.

I climbed on top of one of the dug-outs to thank the fans in the main stand – 1,710 turned out despite bad weather – and then went over to the Fletcher Street End. They responded with chants of "Fozzie is a Wire". I threw my shirt, yellow boots, pads and – as I had promised – my primrose and blue gum shield into the Fletcher End. Someone might still have the boots, but I cannot imagine that anyone has kept the gum shield. I told reporters: "The score was immaterial, it was just very emotional to think that was the last time I would be playing in front of the people who I have shared many happy moments with during my time at Warrington. You can take the boy out of the primrose and blue but you can't take the primrose and blue out of the boy. I still live in Warrington, although I'm playing for Widnes, I've got a business here and all my family and I'm not moving anywhere. I would love to come back to the club and contribute in one way or another."

Valentine's Day had been a busy time for the testimonial committee. The late Dave Carter was a business partner of mine and his wife ran the Wishing Well florists. We arranged that Warrington players would deliver flowers to wives or girlfriends (or both) at no extra charge and they were mad busy. The young lads were taking out three or four bunches at a time and they loved it and the young ladies loved it too. We should have produced a calendar like they do now. We organised a murder mystery night at the Village Hotel, but none of the players – being thick as normal – guessed whodunit or what the weapon was. We also had a St Patrick's night ceilidh at Tetley Walker's club. Angela Powers, from Sky Sports, hosted the final gala dinner. The secret to having a good testimonial year is to have a good committee who are prepared to work hard and help as much as they can. Thankfully, my committee were and I cannot thank them enough. My second testimonial year did even better than my first and raised £36,000.

Mark's second testimonial match at Wilderspool, 2001

Mark in the dressing room before the match with his team and children Chris, Dan and Beckie.

Mark with a blood-stained shirt at the end of the match.

Mark at the end of the match with supporters showing their appreciation.
(All photos: courtesy Forster family)

Left: The brochure for Mark's second testimonial.

12. Irish eyes

Super League World Nines
22–24 February 1996, National Stadium, Suva City, Fiji

Ireland manager Terry Flanagan, from Oldham, rang me up out of the blue and said: "Foz, we are going to Fiji. Have you got any Irish ancestors?" I said: "Terry, I'll find out and I'll ring you back in two minutes." I put the phone down and rang my mum up and asked her. "Yes," she said. "Your granddad Ernest Jennings. What are you up to? You are always up to something." I said I would tell her later. I rang Terry back and told him the news and he said: "Do you fancy going to Fiji for three weeks?" I said I'd love to. It was just as all the News International money was coming into Super League. The Ireland squad included James Lowes and Craig McElhatton, from Bradford Bulls, Leo Casey, from Featherstone Rovers, Tony Nuttall, from Oldham Bears, and myself. We met at the Thistle Hotel in Haydock and the RFL, in their infinite wisdom, gave us £100 expenses each to get to London, stop overnight and get on the 6am flight to Fiji. So that led to the biggest game of cards we've ever had. Some guys lost all of their money.

Once we got to Fiji, we were given £75 a day. A three-course meal in Fiji only cost £4.50 and so if we weren't training we played cards. All week. We weren't allowed to go out. We stopped in the same hotel as England, Scotland and Tonga and, on the first day after training, we were around the pool and I decided to sunbathe for 20 minutes. I got third degree burns and was taken off to hospital. They said it was one of the worst cases of sunburn they had seen. The sweat on my body after training must have boiled and I got covered in blisters and that was before day one of the tournament. They gave me this fantastic cream – I wish I had some now – and that sorted me out. But in the matches every time I made a tackle a blister would burst and fluid would be running down my arms. I had to have a cold bath after every match just to get my shirt off because it had stuck to me. For the record, we beat France 16–12 and Japan 20–4, but lost to Western Samoa 32–18, Tonga 36–8 and New Zealand, the eventual winners, 20–0. We finished eighth out of the 16 nations.

Steve O'Neill, the former Widnes prop, was appointed Ireland coach in 1997 and he had a pub in Widnes called the Appleton Arms. When we went over to Dublin Steve would collect all our boarding passes. We didn't know what he was doing, but he would then buy 200 packets of fags to sell in his bar. He was a character and we used to call him 'Square Head' – behind his back obviously.

Ralph Rimmer took over as manager and on one trip to Dublin he said that if the players helped with unloading the bags we could have free beer for a few rounds. So obviously we did, especially those with partners and family with us. Then Ralph fell asleep in the hotel and we kept his tab open all night and he ended up with a bill for about £1,000. Ralph was a great bloke and just paid it. Some of the younger lads had gone into

Dublin and spent a fortune. When they came back to the hotel they asked us how much money we'd spent. "Nothing," came the reply.

France 30 Ireland 30
Tuesday, 13 May, 1997, Stade Robert Bobin, Evry-Bondoufle, Paris
This was my full Ireland debut, aged 32. It was the first time France and Ireland had played a full international and what a match it was. We were losing 30–16 with 25 minutes left, but then launched an incredible fightback. Bradford hooker James Lowes scored a try, I scored a try and, finally, St Helens stand-off Tommy Martyn scored a try. Dublin Blues winger Phelim Comerford kicked the goal and we had salvaged a draw. Two former Warrington team-mates joined me in the Ireland team, Huddersfield prop Neil Harmon and Oldham scrum-half Martin Crompton, who was our captain. A future Warrington team-mate Jerome Guisset was on the bench for France. Poor Tommy Martyn, who was the man-of-the-match, suffered a serious knee injury near the end.

Ireland 22 France 24
Wednesday, 4 November 1998, Tolka Park, Dublin, Tri- Nations Championship
By now, Shaun Edwards was 32 and playing for the London Broncos. He had also discovered an Irish grandparent and made his Ireland debut in this match, scoring two tries. I played in the centre; Martin Crompton was the captain and loose-forward. At the other end of the scale, a 22-year-old winger from the Dublin Blues club, by the name of Brian Carney, also made his Ireland debut. We were leading 22–14 midway through the second half, but France snatched victory in the last minute.

Scotland 10 Ireland 17
Wednesday, 18 November, 1998, Firhill Park, Partick Thistle FC, Glasgow
Tri-Nations Championship
Lee Penny and Jason Roach were playing for Scotland and I was playing for Ireland – six days before my 34th birthday. We were already back in pre-season training with Warrington and, before we left, Darryl van de Velde called us together and told us: "Whatever you do, don't injure each other." Jason was on the right wing for Scotland, Lee was the full-back and I was on the left wing for Ireland. Late on in the match I was charging for the corner and I could see both of them racing in to tackle me like demons. So I dived for the corner – and scored the match-winning try – and they smashed into each other and knocked each other out. Of course, I got the blame, but I told Darryl that if I hadn't dived all three of us would have been knocked out. We all shook hands after the game, there was no malice in it, partied that night and returned to Warrington training the next day. There were actually four Warrington players in the Scotland team: Lee, Jason, scrum-half John Duffy and loose-forward Mike Wainwright and they were coached by another former Warrington player in Billy McGinty. But we had three Wigan players playing for us – centre Gary Connolly, prop Terry O'Connor and second row Mick Cassidy – and

Terry was the man-of-the-match. It was a cold, wet, miserable night and only 1,000 people turned out to watch us. Ireland coach Steve O'Neill said: "We are sowing the seeds and raising the awareness of the game in both countries. We will keep chiselling away and are determined to show people that rugby league will not go away in Ireland and Scotland."

Wales 17 Ireland 24
Friday 15 October 1999, Vetch Field, Swansea
Triangular Tournament
Wales were without Iestyn Harris, Keiron Cunningham and Anthony Sullivan, who were on Great Britain duty in Australia, and so Clive Griffiths gave seven youngsters their debuts. Then, after 10 minutes, their second row, Richie Eyres, was sent off. Mick Cassidy, Martin Crompton and Tommy Martyn scored our tries with my opposite winger Ian Herron kicking six goals. As usual, Lee Briers kicked a drop-goal for Wales.

Ireland 31 Scotland 10
Sunday 31 October 1999, Tolka Park, Dublin
Triangular Tournament
I was always a passionate player and didn't like to see older players taking advantage of younger kids, bullying them. By now I was also a senior player, coming to the end of my career, and wanted to look after the younger lads. Sheffield Eagles player Darren Shaw was in the second row for Scotland and I thought he was giving it out a bit too much to the younger lads. So I went in to tackle him quite hard and calm him down. But he lifted his elbow up and caught my forearm on the point of his elbow. Ouch! Seamus McCallion, our physio, came on and said it was only the belly of the muscle and, anyway, there was nobody left on the bench and so I would have to carry on playing. I said "What about those two?" – pointing to Barrie McDermott and Terry O'Connor. Barrie, apparently, had a tight calf. Terry, apparently, had a dead leg. Seamus said: "It's only a bang, you can carry on playing."

So I carried on playing – like rugby league players do – not realising I had broken my arm. I even scored a try. As soon as we came off the pitch, the doctor, Mick Malloy, took me to the local hospital for an X-ray and we went straight to the front of the queue. I said: "Mick, I'm not happy with pushing in." He said it was all right because he was the head doctor. By now my arm was dangling down like a piece of spaghetti. He took the X-ray and said it was one of the worst breaks he had even seen. He gave me two painkillers and put a cast on it so that I could still go out for a drink with the lads.

We had a meal and went round a few bars, but a nightclub wouldn't let me in because of the cast "in case I hurt myself". I said: "Are you taking the mickey?" But they wouldn't have it. Tommy Martyn and Steve Prescott, who were both in the Ireland team at the time, said they wouldn't leave me on my own and so we went to a little pub on the corner. They bought me six pints of lager and six Bacardi and Cokes, after which I was steaming, whereas they didn't seem to be drinking anywhere near as much. Then they put me in a taxi back to the hotel and said: "Right, we can go to the nightclub now!"

I already knew Steve Prescott from playing against him for St Helens and Hull, but playing together for Ireland really cemented our friendship. He was a cracking full-back and it was a pleasure to play on the wing when he was in the side because he was a true athlete and a true gentleman. I remember we took our daughter Beckie to London for her 13th birthday and were queuing up to go on the London Eye when I saw Steve coming off the other side. It was just after he had been diagnosed with a rare form of stomach cancer in 2006 and only given a few months to live. He looked like he had a football shoved up his jumper, but he fought the illness like a champion and raised £500,000 for charity through various challenges with the likes of Paul Sculthorpe. He died, aged 39, in 2013, but his name lives on through the Steve Prescott Foundation.

In 2014 Dr Marwan Koukash, the Salford chairman and racehorse owner, named one of his horses Steve Prescott in his honour and it won its first race at Haydock Park. Dr Koukash delivered an emotional speech and then donated the £3,000 prize money to the Steve Prescott Foundation. I think every rugby league player in the country had backed it to win as well.

Playing for Ireland in the 2000 Rugby League World Cup was one of the highlights of my career. We were in Group Four with Samoa, New Zealand Maori and Scotland and played the opening game of the tournament – against Samoa at Windsor Park in Belfast. We won that 30–16 and then beat Scotland and the New Zealand Maori in Dublin to finish top of our pool. Against the New Zealand Maori I scored the try that was voted the best in the group stages. Tawera Nikau had the ball and ran at me with two more Warrington players in support – Dave Kidwell and Toa Kohe-Love. Three onto one. It should have been a try for the Maori. But, for some reason, 'T' tried to chip the ball over my head. I caught it and raced 90 yards with 'T', Toa and Dave Kidwell chasing me. But there was no way they were going to catch me. After the match, I rang Darryl van der Velde to tell him I had just outstripped three of his players to score a try in the World Cup. I couldn't help myself.

We played England in the quarter-finals at Headingley. For some reason we were based in Sheffield and so we had to travel to Leeds for the match. We got stuck in traffic and were late arriving at the ground. Everything was against us, but we only lost 26–16.

Back in Sheffield after the match the former Ireland coach Steve O'Neill and kitman 'Big Paul' Hansbury got me drunk and then took me to Widnes the following day to see Wales beat Papua New Guinea 22–8 in their quarter-final. I was just going there for a social drink to finish off the World Cup and to watch the game but I ended up signing for Widnes.

Mark welcomes Kevin Campion to the Ireland squad. Campion was supposed to join Warrington after the 2000 Rugby League World Cup but changed his mind.

Mark (third right) and the Ireland team line up before the Rugby League World Cup match against New Zealand Maori in Dublin. (Both photos: Mike Boden, *Warrington Guardian*).

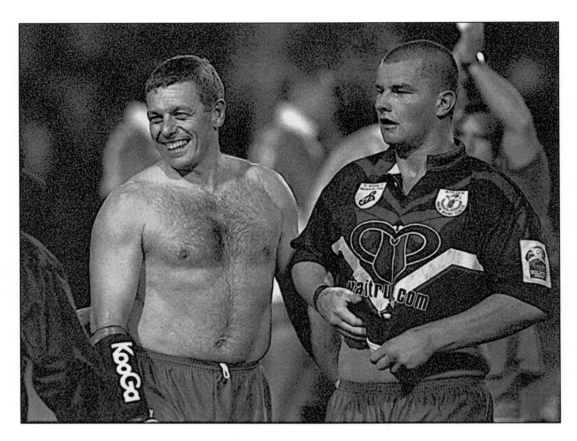

Mark celebrates the victory over New Zealand Maori
(Photo: Mike Boden, *Warrington Guardian*)

13. Widnes gum shield

Doug Laughton, the former Widnes coach, famously described David and Paul Hulme as 'The Brothers Grimm' – but playing against them was no fairy tale. In fact, it was a horror story. David was a half-back while Paul was a hooker or second row and they both played for Great Britain. Paul Bishop, the Warrington scrum-half, said one of the brothers would be biting you, one would be pinching you and one would be punching you and you couldn't work out which was which. He was exaggerating, of course, but they took the game right to the edge and I don't think they would get away with it now with video referees and the like. Paul Bishop and Paul Hulme were sent off for fighting in the John Player Special Trophy semi-final at Central Park in December 1986. Both players were banned for two matches which meant that Bish missed the final. Off the field 'The Brothers Grimm' were both fantastic company. Paul spent two seasons with me at Warrington – 1996 and 1997 – while I took my coaching badge with David, who was the Widnes head coach when I joined them in November 2000.

Tony Chambers was the Widnes chairman and he printed off my contract in his office on Wednesday 15 November – nine days before my 36th birthday. I checked it through, pushed it back to him and we discussed a particular issue I was concerned about. Tony said he had heard of players wanting cars or houses, but never rejecting a contract because of the issue I raised.

I had done quite well in the World Cup and was a Super League player going down to the Northern Ford Premiership. It was a big signing for the club and there was a big announcement in the town. When I made my debut for Widnes against Whitehaven at the Auto Quest Stadium on Sunday, 3 December we went out as a team, did the warm-up, got a great reception and went back to the dressing room. Then I put my gum shield in as normal and went out again for the match and stood on the wing. This time some fans started booing and shouting and calling me. This went on for about two or three games. Eventually I went over to the fans and asked them why they were jeering me. They said it was because I was still wearing a primrose and blue gum shield. For the following game I got a black and white gum shield instead and they all cheered me. That was the level of passion between Warrington and Widnes and that's why not too many players have played successfully for both. There are probably only Rick Thackray, Jonathan Davies, Kevin Tamati, Andy Gregory, Tony Thorniley and me in recent times.

But the rivalry cuts both ways. After my first game for Widnes I had a meal with the players to celebrate. We had beaten Whitehaven, who were being coached by Paul Cullen, 22–14 and I had scored a try on my debut. Another old friend, half-back Martin Crompton, had come on as a substitute for his debut and created three of our five tries. After that I went home early to find that some Warrington supporters had egged my house in Woolston. It didn't look very good and by the following morning, when I came to clean it up, the egg was rock hard on all the windows. It took me forever to wash it off. The fans obviously thought I'd walked out on Warrington to join Widnes, which wasn't the case.

We were the favourites to win promotion to Super League and won our second match too, 24–14 at Rochdale, before we suffered two defeats over the Christmas period. We lost 25–20 at home to Leigh on Boxing Day when the crowd at the Auto Quest Stadium was an impressive 6,644 and then lost 20–12 against Oldham at Boundary Park on New Year's Day. The Leigh game was interesting because their full-back was the 21-year-old Neil Turley, whose father Norman had had the fight with me at Wilderspool during my first trial match almost 20 years earlier. Also around this time I played an 'A' team game for Widnes with Chris Kelly – Ken Kelly's son – and that did make me feel old.

We began 2001 with a 26–16 victory over Workington and I scored the opening try after two minutes. It was the 199th try of my career. Our scrum-half Ian Watson had a bit of a nightmare with his goalkicking. He missed seven kicks at goal – six conversions and a penalty – before he finally kicked a penalty from in front of the posts in the last minute and received a huge, ironic cheer.

The Northern Ford Premiership was playing a half-winter/half-summer season and, inevitably, we had some games postponed because of frozen pitches. We earned a 6–6 draw on a snow-covered pitch at Barrow. After five seasons of playing summer rugby in Super League, it was something of a culture shock.

Another old friend was waiting for me in the third round of the Silk Cut Challenge Cup when Widnes were drawn at home to the amateur side Wigan St Patrick's who were being coached by Andy Gregory. My best man was not expecting any favours from us and did not get any as we won 70–2 with hooker Phil Cantillon scoring four of our 13 tries. The fourth-round draw sent us to face the Bradford Bulls at Valley Parade. The Bradford team included Henry and Robbie Paul at half-back, Tevita Vaikona on one wing, a front row of Brian McDermott, James Lowes and Stuart Fielden, a young Jamie Peacock in the second row, with Big Joe Vagana and Paul Anderson on the bench. We did not stand a chance, but put up a good effort before losing 54–10.

Seven days later, on Sunday 18 February, I scored the 200th try of my career in injury time at the end of a farcical home match against York. Three of the York players had failed to show up because of a dispute about money and so Lee Crooks, their coach, put himself on the substitutes' bench. I was 36 and he was 37, but he hadn't played for four years. He was joined on the bench by his kit man Steve Harris and physio Pat Howdle. Lee had to bring himself on for 25 minutes in the second half. It was all too easy and we won 90–6, with hooker Phil Cantillon scoring seven tries. It was a record win for Widnes and a record defeat for York. I scored in injury time, but didn't realise it was my 200th try until somebody told me after the match. Wins at Chorley and Gateshead followed but then, in March, we lost two games in a row – against Sheffield at the Don Valley Stadium and at home to Doncaster Dragons. Frustratingly, I was a non-playing sub on both occasions. David Hulme was sacked as head coach the following Tuesday after just a year in charge.

Mark signed for Widnes Vikings in November 2000. (Photo: courtesy Forster family)

Widnes turned to Neil Kelly who had enjoyed five successful years in charge of the Dewsbury Rams and results improved almost straight away. Neil's first official game in charge was against Hunslet at the Auto Quest Stadium on Sunday, 1 April. I played on the wing, Martin Crompton was the captain and we won 64–6. The following week we beat Neil's old team, the Dewsbury Rams, 13–12 at the Ram Stadium. We lost at Leigh on Good Friday, but then beat Oldham at home on Easter Monday in a remarkable match. We were losing 16–6 at half-time, but scored 28 unanswered points in the second half to win 34–16. Whatever Neil said at half-time obviously worked and we were named the Northern Ford Premiership team of the month for April.

My arm injury was now causing me some grief and I was rested for the next match at home to Hull KR when we won 28–0, but I was back in the team for the trip to Paul Cullen's Whitehaven on Sunday 6 May. Unusually for Whitehaven, the sun was shining and we were winning. Then, with about 10 seconds left, I scooted from behind a scrum. I was tackled from the side and my knee gave way and I needed minor surgery. I did not realise it at the time, but that would prove to be my final game for Widnes. I was out for a few weeks before I got the all-clear to train again, which I was really looking forward to. I even did some gym work and I'm not a great fan of that.

Steve O'Neill, who was then the joint Ireland coach with Andy Kelly, rang me to ask if I was available to play for Ireland against France in Albi. I said I had not played for Widnes for seven weeks but, if they agreed, I'd love to. Steve spoke to the Widnes committee and they agreed and Neil Kelly, the Widnes coach, agreed because he wanted me match fit for the play-offs.

France 56 Ireland 16
Tuesday 26 June, 2001, Stade Municipal, Albi
Warrington's Rob Smyth was on one wing and I was on the other. He was knocked out after two or three minutes and was soon sat on the bench with a big bag of ice on his head. I was having a good game, I was busy and my knee was holding up and I scored a try – the 201st of my career. Then I made a break and was tackled by their full-back, Renaud Guigue. A French forward fell on my left ankle and tore the ligaments on either side of the joint and the one that joins across it. A bit of bone was pulled away too. I hobbled off in agony and sat next to Rob with my foot in a bucket of iced water. Not surprisingly, we lost. I saw a specialist over in France and one back in England. I was told it would have been better if I had broken my leg and my ankle. That was it. My professional career at international level and club level was over after almost 20 years and 491 games.

When we played an international match we were always insured. There was supposed to be a £50,000 pay-out if someone's career was ended by injury. I got in touch with the insurers and the RFL and it turned into a massive discussion and fall-out. They did not want to pay me the £50,000 because my contract at Widnes wasn't worth that much. Luckily, I was a member of the players' union, the Rugby League Players' Association. Andy

Goodway was the chairman and I got in touch with him. We met for a coffee and I told him I didn't want to give rugby league a bad name, but I wanted the pay-out I was owed. I was married with three kids and couldn't work because of the injury. I gave him all the facts and the contracts and he said he would sort it out.

Andy was true to his word. In the meantime, Widnes gave me £1,500 and the RFL deducted that from the £50,000. At first, the RFL offered me a quarter of the pay-out. Then, because I had been a good servant to the game, they offered me half. Andy did all the talking and insisted I receive the full amount. The RLPA really got their teeth into it and got barristers involved. They said it would wreck any future players' chances of getting a full pay-out if I accepted less and so I pushed for the full amount and got it. Eventually.

Without me, Widnes finished second in the Northern Ford Premiership behind Leigh and then beat Rochdale Hornets and Leigh in the play-offs to reach the Grand Final against Oldham at Spotland in July. Widnes looked after me fantastically well and I went on the team bus to the Grand Final and had the meal beforehand. They even made me a replica shirt with '5' and 'Forster' on the back and I got a winners' medal. Widnes won a thrilling match 24–14 and had won a place in Super League. I was proud to have played my part. Phil Cantillon was the man-of-the-match in the Grand Final. He was a cracking lad and had an amazing engine. Hookers now do 20 or 25 minutes, but Cant played the full 80. He had trained himself to maximum fitness. He must have been the fittest semi-professional player and his try-scoring record was incredible. That season he scored 48 tries, a world record for a forward.

Also in July, I found myself pictured on the front page of the *Widnes World* under the headline "Rugby hero is on the ball in gas rescue: Widnes Vikings star is hailed a lifesaver after dragging man clear of toxic leak" – which was all a bit embarrassing. I was working for a company called North Supplies, selling glasses and toiletries and the like to the pub trade, and called at the Adelphi Vaults in Warrington. I needed the barman, Frank Lenihan, to sign for the delivery, but couldn't find him, which was a bit odd. I went into the cellar to look for him and found him lying semi-conscious on the floor, overcome by fumes. A gas pipe must have come loose and the smell was terrible. I picked him up and carried him over my shoulder and out onto the street where he eventually came round from his ordeal. And do you know what? I never even got a free pint for it! Harold Lynskey, the Widnes secretary, said: "We are very proud of Mark for what he did. His only concern was to get Mr Lenihan to safety. If he hadn't helped him who knows what could have happened."

I only started 13 games for Widnes and must have picked up 13 injuries, but I can still ring them up now and the girls in the office recognise my voice. They ask me if I am coming to a match and bringing the kids or the grandkids. They always looked after me at Widnes. At the end of the season, Neil Kelly said to me: "Foz, you have been a great servant but I can't give you another contract." I said: "Neil, I've had that many injuries I don't want another contract." We shook hands and have been great friends ever since.

After that I decided to let my body recover a bit and just carried on coaching at Rylands. After 12 months or so I had piled the weight on and gone up to 18 stones from my ideal playing weight of 15 stones and it didn't really suit me, just barking out orders in the middle of a training field. I started to train a bit and that was it. I started being a named substitute to make the numbers up, and then came on for 10 minutes up in Cumbria, aged 37, then came on for 20 minutes, then half a game, then a full game. I had got the bug again. After that I regretted not being able to go around the lower divisions in the professional game, division one and division two, and going on to make 500 appearances as a professional.

The 2005–06 season was one of the most successful and enjoyable of my entire career. I was the Rylands head coach and playing in the centres for the first team – aged 41 and 42. We won the North West Counties Cup for the first time in 110 years and lifted the North West Counties Division One title. I was also shortlisted for the Warrington Sports Personality of 2006 award, in a competition organised by the *Warrington Guardian*. Also on the shortlist were golfer Paul Slater, footballer Alex Dunne, kickboxer Graham Sayer and canoeist Jon Akinyemi. The awards night was held at the Halliwell Jones Stadium.

I also played for the BARLA Bulldogs international veterans team in over-35s competitions, including the Dubai Sevens which are played in November. It was freezing back home but, between matches, we were sunbathing around a pool. Jason Robinson was there in 2011 as an ambassador for HSBC and was stripped to the waist and still toned. I asked him if he was playing, but he said he had let himself go. He only had a five pack instead of a six pack. But he had obviously got the taste for it and the following year he played for the Joining Jack charity, set up by the former Wigan player Andy Johnson to raise money for research into Duchenne Muscular Dystrophy. His son, Jack, has the condition.

The Joining Jack team was full of stars. Andy Johnson was the captain and as well as Jason Robinson they had Kris Radlinski, Sean Long, Gary Connolly, Martin Offiah, Steve Hampson, BJ Mather, Denis Betts, Mick Cassidy, Paul Sculthorpe, Steve Blakeley and Brian Carney plus the then Warrington captain Adrian Morley.

The BARLA Bulldogs weren't household names in our own households. As well as me there were David Wynne, Paul Dean, Thomas McKinnon, Kevin Hetherington, Michael Ward, Sean Richardson, Stephen Bird, Stephen Morton, Lee Kelley, Adam Hoyle, James Walker, Christopher Peach, Kieran Kavanagh and Sean Caley. But both teams were unbeaten in the group stages and so met in the quarter-finals.

Against all odds we took the lead after two minutes when good work from Steve Bird of Bank Quay Bulls, Sean Richardson and Kieran Kavanagh gave me the chance to score – a few days before my 48th birthday. It got a bit heated after that and Jimmy Walker was sent to the sin bin. Steve Blakeley, the former Salford and Warrington half-back, then scored for Joining Jack to make the half-time score 5–5.

We defended magnificently in the second half, but could not stop Kris Radlinski and Steve Blakeley scoring further tries for Joining Jack. Sean Long and Jimmy Walker had a bit of a scuffle and Adrian Morley was sin-binned for complaining about an alleged elbow. It was all good, clean fun and gave us plenty to talk about around the pool later.

Mick Turner, our manager, said: "I was a proud man today. Our lads gave their heart and soul and were unlucky to lose. This was great coverage for the Joining Jack charity."

I re-signed for the Woolston Rovers first team in the 2015 January transfer window – aged 50. Not surprisingly, there was no one near my age in the team. The nearest one was Mike Ward who was 36 and he said he felt old. The rest were all kids, but I enjoyed it. I always promised that I would go back to Woolston and have a couple of seasons there before I finally retired. Woolston was where it all started for me and they looked after me when I was a young lad and now they were looking after me at a very old age.

My former Warrington team-mate John Fieldhouse was the first team coach. He knew what I could do and I knew what he wanted from me. Woolston had been asking me to go back for two or three years. First of all they asked me to coach, but I told them I still wanted to play. So I helped John out, helped the second-team coach out and played whenever I wanted to or whenever I could. That suited me with my job.

I never thought when I retired as a professional aged 36 in 2001 that I would still be playing as an amateur 14 years later. I had left Woolston to sign for Warrington when I was 15 and returned 35 years later. My first game back was a friendly against Wigan St Patrick's – who had wanted to sign me 36 years earlier – and that ended in a draw.

My first league game was at Oldham St Anne's and we lost by four points after running out of fit players after picking up a few injuries. I got a few strange looks when we pulled up at Oldham because they thought I was the coach. I bumped into Mick Worrall, the former Oldham forward, who was out walking his dog and he asked me: "What are you doing here?" St Anne's was a ground I liked going to because the crowd were very close to the players and we could have a bit of banter with them. John Fieldhouse played me in the centre and the second row. I did 70 minutes as prop against Bury Bears once because nobody else wanted to do it. Whatever position you play, rugby league is a great game and a wonderful way of keeping fit.

Left: Mark takes time out during Rylands's successful 2005–06 season, when he was the club's player-coach

Below: Mark playing for Rylands in a cup game.

(Both photos: Mike Boden, *Warrington Guardian*)

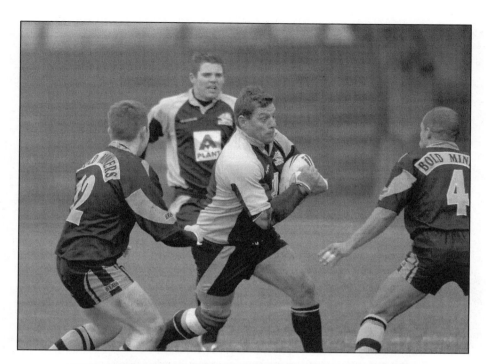

Two pictures of Mark playing for Rylands against Bold Miners from St Helens.
(Photos: Mike Boden, *Warrington Guardian*)

Mark with sons Dan (right) and Chris after winning the Lancashire Cup with Bank Quay Bulls by beating West Bank at Leigh Miners.

Mark playing for Bank Quay Bulls against Wigan St Cuthberts as his 50th birthday approaches. (Both photos: Mike Boden, *Warrington Guardian*).

14. Referees and reflections

I am a rugby league man through and through. I don't even support an association football team. If it is on in the pub and is a conversational thing I will watch it, but I won't go out of my way to watch. But I have been lucky enough to play at Elland Road, Old Trafford and Anfield and see behind the scenes at those famous grounds and not many football fans can say that.

Times have changed. When I started playing, matches were normally on Sunday afternoons and I would have a Chinese meal the night before. Then, on the morning of the match, I would eat steak, tinned spaghetti and a poached egg, followed by rice pudding. I would eat that at about 10.30am for a 3pm kick-off. We were told that gave you plenty of time to digest it, but it probably gave us longer for it to lie on our stomachs. After a few years, we were told to drop the steak and replace it with tuna and a few years after that we were told to drop the rice pudding. So then it was just tuna, tinned spaghetti and a poached egg.

Playing cards was a big thing in rugby league. I remember I was on a team coach to Cumbria once when the late Warrington winger Mike Kelly lost his three-piece suite. He had the money in his pocket to pay for the suite and was going to do it before he boarded the coach, but was running late. He obviously thought he could buy a better three-piece suite if he played cards – and won – but he lost the lot, probably £300 back then, and we got beaten as well.

Brian Pitchford, the Warrington chairman, used to walk down the team coach from his seat at the front. One day he saw us playing cards and said: "Are you gambling? I don't pay you good money to gamble it all away. You need to start playing for Jelly Babies." So we did. We started playing for Jelly Babies and Midget Gems, but we didn't tell Mr Pitchford that a Midget Gem was worth 50p and a Jelly Baby was worth £1. Mr Pitchford was a fantastic chairman and looked after everyone and, as chairman of Locker Industries, employed quite a few players as well.

Mike Kelly died in March 2011 and it was only then that we found out he had been misleading everyone about his age for more than 30 years. When he signed for Warrington from Crosfields in 1977, Mike said he was 22 – rather than 25 – because he did not think that Alex Murphy would want to sign a 25-year-old and he was probably right. So Mike was 59 when he died, not 56.

My favourite singer is the American singer-songwriter Tracy Chapman, who had a worldwide smash hit with her single *Fast Car* in 1988. I used to listen to her CDs when I was driving to a match. It got me in the zone. A lot of people have asked me why and I think it was the lyrics. They are all about going through hard times. I have always been pretty lucky, was paid quite well to play a sport I loved and so her lyrics kept my feet on the ground. I kept her CDs in the car and before my kids could count to 10 they could sing Tracy Chapman songs. I went to see her when she was on tour, at the Manchester Apollo.

After Catalans Dragons joined Super League in 2006 I travelled to Perpignan to watch Warrington play. I was sitting in the square, outside the castle, where everybody meets for a drink, when a female voice said: "You don't recognise me, do you Foz?" It was Marie Jenkins, John Woods's former wife, who was living in the south of France with her new husband Paul, who was from Howley, where I grew up. People say that rugby league is a family and they are right. We now visit them in the south of France and go out for a meal with them when they come back to Warrington.

In the early days my favourite referees were Fred Lindop from Wakefield and Ronnie Campbell from Widnes. I could give somebody a dig off the ball and he would give me one back and the referee would say on the run: "I saw that. That's one all. Any more of it and I'll deal with it." The referees were always very fair like that. They were only doing it as a part-time job; we were part-time and had the utmost respect for them. As a young kid we didn't dare call the referee. The referee would get onto a player who did, their coach would get on to the player and, worst of all, the captain and senior players would get on to him. They would say "We don't talk to referees like that."

Later on, a little fat kid from St Helens – commonly known as Steve Ganson – was a top referee as well and I have done a few sportsman's dinners with him and we have a great craic. The Connolly brothers from Wigan, Bob and John, were both referees and I never knew which was which but it didn't really matter because I thought they both didn't like me because I was fast, elusive and very, very cheeky. After the rule was introduced banning ball stealing in a two-man tackle, I was playing in a match at Wilderspool and took the ball away from the Fletcher End. Bob was the referee, although it might have been John. The ball was ripped out in a two-man tackle and I shouted "Sir" and put two fingers up to indicate there were two men in the tackle. He stopped play, pulled me to one side and said: "I am going to penalise you for abusing the referee, for putting two fingers up. Penalty against Warrington." I said: "Sir, it was a two-man tackle. They've stolen the ball off me." "Oh yes, Foz," he admitted, realising his mistake. "We'll keep that between ourselves. Penalty against Warrington." So Bob or John, whichever, the secret's out.

The Warrington referee Karl Kirkpatrick gave me stick for years about being offside. When the referee's back was towards me, I would always sneak half a yard, it's human nature. But when the referees got mic-ed up to the touch judges all that changed. Without turning around, Karl used to say: "Foz, I can see you're offside behind me." I said: "Why, have you got eyes in the back of your head?" The touch judge had obviously told him. Later on, Karl was refereeing me at Widnes and then he wasn't mic-ed up. But once again, without turning around, Karl said: "Foz, I know you are offside." I said to him: "That's impossible. I know you are not mic-ed up at this level." He agreed and said: "True, but I still know you are offside." And he was right.

In 2007, Karl became the first referee in the professional game to switch codes. He had turned down a full-time contract with Super League because he did not want to give up his job with the Royal Bank of Scotland. After that, he couldn't referee Super League games anymore or take charge of major finals and so he switched codes. These days he is a very funny after-dinner speaker and starts his routine with the following line: "My name is Karl Kirkpatrick and I am a referee and I am a banker. Yes, you heard that correctly, a banker with a 'b'." That gets the audience on his side straight away.

He also tells a funny story about the difference between rugby union and rugby league. He was taking charge of a union game at Stockport RUFC who were playing Preston Grasshoppers. The former St Helens player Sean Long was playing for Preston. Before kick-off Karl and the players had a walk-about on the pitch. Sean approached Karl and complained that there was some dog shit on the 20m line and wanted it removed. Karl then went to see the club secretary or chairman and told him about the problem. The official walked over and examined the offending pile and said: "That's not dog shit, it's badger shit." Apologies for repeating some of your material, Karl, but you shouldn't have kept penalising me for being offside should you?

I bump into referees in the most unlikely places. I was out with some friends in Liverpool in 2013 and stood outside Smokie Mo's bar, minding my own business, when a voice said: "Hello Foz." It was Richard Silverwood, wearing a very fetching pink T-shirt. I said to him: "That's a lovely pink T-shirt you're wearing Richard." He said: "It's not pink, it's salmon." I said: "It's not salmon, it's pink." This went on for a while, with us both sticking to our guns, before we went our separate ways.

Later that year, Samoa played Fiji at the Halliwell Jones Stadium during the Rugby League World Cup and, as a former Warrington player who had played for Ireland in the World Cup, I was asked to walk out onto the pitch alongside both teams, carrying the match ball ready for kick-off. Some of those Fijians and Samoans were enormous. I was concentrating on making sure the lettering on the ball was the right way round and not slipping over because the pitch was a bit wet. As I got closer to the centre of the pitch I looked up. Guess who was the referee? None other than Richard Silverwood.

Obviously, I wasn't mic-ed up, but Richard was. When I got to about 10 yards away from him I said: "Richard, very striking kit, and not pink like last time I saw you." His two touch judges and two in-goal judges turned around and started to smirk. I continued: "Yes, it was in Liverpool, wasn't it Richard? And you were wearing a lovely pink T-shirt." So Richard, without moving his lips and through gritted teeth, said: "It was flipping salmon." By now the two touch judges and two in-goal judges were dying to laugh and Richard said: "I will get you back for this."

The following year I was in the airport going to Egypt to celebrate my 50th birthday and, again, I heard this voice behind me: "I told you I would get you back." It was Richard Silverwood and we had a good laugh about it all. I thought about that story again when the NRL season started in Australia in 2015 and the referees refused to wear pink because they thought it undermined their authority. Perhaps they should have worn salmon instead.

People often ask me to pick the best Warrington team out of all the players I played with and it is not an easy thing to do. At full-back, I could choose from Steve Hesford, Brian Johnson and Lee Penny. Steve could kick a ball as high as anybody and as far as anybody and still be down the other end of the field before it bounced, but I would have to pick Johnno and hope that somebody else could kick the goals.

On the wings I would pick myself and Des Drummond. John Bevan was a brilliant winger, but he had moved into the centre by the time I started playing. I had dozens of centres, John, Paul Cullen, Ronnie Duane, Gary Mercer, Jonathan Davies and Allan Bateman were all excellent.

Paul Cullen was as hard as nails. He celebrated his testimonial season in 1990–91 and I remember writing in his testimonial brochure: "I was at Woolston when Paul was at Crosfields. But fortunately I didn't play against him, or I might not be here today." Ronnie Duane tells me now in the pub that he always looked after me and made my name. He would get a good hiding, go between the winger and centre and pop the ball over and I would finish them off. I just say that he was too slow to finish them off himself. We trained together, played together and worked together. Gary was a New Zealand international at full-back, wing and second row and a very good player. I knew what he was going to do all the time, unlike with Jonathan Davies. I didn't have a clue what Jiffy was going to do. Allan Bateman won three caps for Great Britain and 12 for Wales. He was very quick over the first 10 yards and then would be looking for me on the outside to finish it off. Again, it is a very difficult choice, but I think I would probably go with Mercer and Bateman.

At stand-off, I am again spoilt for choice – Ken Kelly (a Man of Steel), Lee Briers (a Lance Todd Trophy winner) and Kelly Shelford (a New Zealand international) – but Ken just edges it. I played with some really good scrum-halves as well, including Andy Gregory, Greg Mackey, Paul Bishop and Martin Crompton. But for his all-round skill I would probably go for Greg Mackey.

Picking the pack is a little bit easier. Obviously, I am not going to go far wrong with a front row of Les Boyd, Kevin Tamati and Bob Jackson, with Steve Molloy and Neil Harmon just missing out as props. Roger O'Mahony was a cracking hooker in the days when scrums were contested. I could put Gary Mercer in the second row, but I think I would have to go with Billy McGinty and Mark Roberts, with Mike Gregory at loose-forward. They were a fantastic back row with an amazing work rate and they all looked after each other, on and off the field.

Ellery Hanley and Shaun Edwards were probably the two best players I played against. Ellery Hanley was the all-round superstar. He was ahead of his time and he was a fitness freak. He would still hold his own in today's game. Shaun Edwards could too because he could read a game and learnt a lot off Ellery Hanley and Andy Gregory. But then I respect anybody who is brave enough to put a rugby league shirt on.

Sadly, some of my Warrington team-mates are no longer with us. Mike Gregory died in November 2007, aged just 43, from progressive muscular atrophy, a form of motor neurone disease, and I went to his funeral. It was like Warrington Walking Day. There was a fantastic turnout. People had to be invited to be in the church, the Sacred Heart, in Springfield, Wigan. It was a great privilege to be there. Former players had come from all over the country to be there – Wales, Scotland, Yorkshire, Humberside and Lancashire. I could have picked a Great Britain team from those present.

Paul Darbyshire, another member of the Warrington team at Wembley in 1990, died in June 2011, aged just 41, also from motor neurone disease, and I went to his funeral too. The service was at St Elphin's Parish Church in Warrington and 55 lads came over from Munster, where Paul had been working as head of strength and conditioning for the previous four years for their rugby union team. Ronan O'Gara, Paul McCarthy and Brian Carney were among the pall bearers and O'Gara and Munster captain Paul O'Connell later delivered eulogies. John Thursfield also paid an emotional tribute.

Dave Chisnall, who had been sin-binned on the day I made my debut at Barrow in 1983, died after a battle with cancer and Alzheimer's Disease, aged 64, in January 2013. As well as playing for Warrington (twice), he had played for Leigh (twice), St Helens, Barrow, England and Great Britain. There was a minute's applause in his memory before the opening Super League game of the season against Castleford.

Greg Mackey, who had the heart of an elephant, never mind the heart of a lion, died in Australia from bowel cancer in July 2014, aged just 52. Gaynor and I went to a benefit dinner at the Halliwell Jones Stadium to celebrate his life and raise money for his family. Ockher – aka Roy Aspinall – the lovable rogue of a Warrington kit man died in January 2014, aged 76, and Alex Murphy spoke at his funeral, again at St Elphin's.

Another death that shocked the whole of rugby league was that of the Great Britain hooker Terry Newton, who took his own life, aged just 31, in September 2010. Terry almost joined Warrington from Wigan St Judes as a teenager and I followed his career with Leeds, Wigan and Bradford closely after that. Terry always played from the heart. Players become used to being in the public eye – the club car, the free meals, the free drinks and the invitations to everywhere – and then, all of a sudden, their career is over and it stops. They are stacking shelves at Asda or on the dole or whatever – I was lucky I had a trade to go back to – and depression can set in. Thankfully, the RFL is aware of the problem and has started the State of Mind programme to help players in need of support.

Finally, in January, Brian Johnson, the former Warrington full-back and coach, died in Australia, aged 59, after a long battle with Alzheimer's Disease. I had known for some time that he was ill but it still came as a shock. He was a brilliant full-back and far-sighted coach. He and his wife Karen introduced a crèche at Wilderspool for players' kids and created a family club. That togetherness and team spirit helped us to be successful on the pitch. All the players I have mentioned above will be sorely missed.

* * * * *

I am often asked if I have any advice for young players just starting out in the game. I always say knuckle down and work hard, but also enjoy yourselves and your moment in the spotlight. The game is a lot more serious now than when I started, but as a young man players still need to have a little bit of fun. They cannot be 100 per cent focused all the time, 24/7 and need to switch off now and again. They will make mistakes, everybody does in every walk of life, but will learn from them, from people around them and their opponents. They shouldn't take mistakes to heart. Try to be better than the player they are playing against. If a youngster manages that their team is one thirteenth of the way to winning the match. If all their mates can beat their opponents too – or the vast majority of them can – then they will win more games than they lose.

A saying that was drummed into me was "satisfy the man in the mirror". The man in the mirror, obviously, is yourself and you can't lie to him. He knows you too well. If you are happy with your game then that is enough. You are bound to be criticised but don't let it get to you. When game plans were introduced, for example, I suffered some criticism from supporters. The pitch was split into zones A, B and C. When the ball was in the air I would catch it and the half-back, be it Ken Kelly or Paul Bishop, would shout "B" and so I ran towards the centre of the field when supporters might have thought that "A" – the wing – was open. But the half-backs had decided I might get pushed into touch and so they shouted "B" and I followed the game plan. Obviously, young players should give rugby league their best shot and, finally, keep their feet on the ground. I kept my feet on the ground because I still worked in the building game. But keep in touch with old friends. I still keep in touch with mine. Youngsters shouldn't lose touch with where they came from because an injury, a couple of bad games, a bad season and they can easily be back there.

In 2012, Andy Gatcliffe, then Warrington's chief executive, rang me up and asked me to go in for a meeting with him. At the meeting, he asked me to host the Mike Gregory Legends lounge on match days and I said I would be delighted. I try to find a player who has played for both clubs and interview them. So when we played Hull I got Alan Hunte, when we played Salford I got Martin Crompton and Tony Thorniley for Widnes. Catalans Dragons was a struggle because there only Jerome Guisset who had played for both clubs and he was busy as part of the Catalan coaching staff and so I got Angela Powers from Sky Sports instead. We always try to predict the score, but we haven't got it right yet.

Trevor Hunt, the radio commentator, always says he is trying to find a past player who hasn't played with me. One week he brought in Jackie Edwards, Warrington's star half-back from the 1950s and 1960s, and said: "There's no way you played with him Foz." I agreed but said I had played with his son Shaun for Lancashire, Great Britain and Ireland.

Alex Murphy looks after the Platinum Club lounge at the other end of the stand and we quite often meet in the middle and have a good chat. I have a lot of respect for Alex. He is still a big personality in the game in his mid–70s. After I had interviewed Alan Hunte for a Hull game he asked me to return the favour for Salford, where he was the head of youth development. There were four tables of Warrington fans there and we had a cracking afternoon, so much so that the Salford chief executive asked me if I would go back for the next home game.

In 2012 I attempted the Three Peaks Challenge, to try to climb the highest mountains in Scotland, England and Wales in 24 hours. It was to raise money for St Rocco's Hospice in Warrington as a tribute to Gaynor's sister, Allison, who was very ill. I do something every year. Ten of us – including Christopher and Daniel – accepted the challenge and set off in a minibus. It picked us up at about 1pm and we drove up to Scotland to tackle Ben Nevis – 4,409 feet – while we were still fresh. The clock starts at the bottom of Ben Nevis. Then it was off to Scafell Pike, 3,209 feet, in Cumbria and, finally, Snowdon at 3,560 feet. Unfortunately, the driver suffered from IBS (irritable bowel syndrome) and so we had to stop at every other service station on the motorway and that slowed us down a bit while he used the toilet. It was funny – at first. We reached the bottom of Snowdon after 24 hours and 20 minutes and so just missed our target.

Dean Fisher, Angela Powers' partner, was parked at the bottom of Snowdon waiting for me and rushed me off to Bradford for a BARLA dinner to collect an open age player of the year award. Gaynor and Angela were already in Bradford, with Allison and her husband Bernie. When we were about 20 minutes away, we received a phone call that Gaynor and Angela had both forgotten to pack our shoes. So we had to stop on the way to buy two pairs of brown shoes, which was surprisingly difficult. I don't think brown shoes are very popular in Bradford. By now my legs were stiff and I could hardly walk. When I finally went up to collect the award I explained what we had been doing, about the Three Peaks Challenge and about our adventure to buy some shoes. There was a huge round of applause and lots of people donated money to St Rocco's.

In 2013, I was featured on the excellent Sky Sports programme *Super League Superstars*. I was interviewed at home by Brian Carney and Sky completely took over the house. There were lights, three cameras and cameramen and we had to rearrange all the furniture. When we were halfway through filming, one of the cameramen went outside for a cigarette or something. It was raining and muddy outside and he walked some mud into the house, although we didn't realise that at the time and carried on filming. After Brian had asked me some more questions, Angela Powers, who was the director, shouted: "Stop! We will have to film all that again." She had seen a muddy footprint on the floor on the film and said: "Gaynor will kill me if there is a muddy footprint in the middle of the shot." So we had to repeat those questions again.

At the end we had to pretend to link in with Sam Tomkins in the studio. I had to focus on a plant and Brian said "Sam Tomkins is that plant" and we just started laughing. Another funny thing happened as well. In the background viewers could see my garden fence and, I didn't realise at the time, but when I painted it I had missed out two slats. After the programme went out two or three days later, my phone was red hot with people saying: "Foz, you could at least have painted your fence properly."

I got a lot of positive feedback as well. A lot of Warrington fans thought I had walked out on the club to join Widnes. They didn't realise that Darryl van de Velde had actually released me. And so that helped to set the record straight.

In May 2014 Mike Nicholas and I were asked by the club to go to the last ever match at Wilderspool: Warrington Wolves Under–16s against Cumbria Regional Academy Under–16s. We walked across the pitch and I said: "I remember scoring this try here or that try over there." Nicko said: "I remember fighting here and getting sent off over there." All the memories started coming back: great games, big crowds, tries, goals, interceptions and injuries. After the match we were even asked to close the gates for the last time. The whole ground has been demolished now, but I have got a little pot of Wilderspool turf at the bottom of my garden. I am going to look after it for as long as I can – and trim it carefully with scissors – a last reminder of a special stadium and a special time in my life.

Another proud day arrived in April 2015 when I was inducted into the Warrington Wolves Hall of Fame during the Warrington Players' Association annual dinner at the Halliwell Jones Stadium. Two of us were inducted that day, both Warrington lads, Alastair Brindle and I. Alastair was a hard-working prop forward who made 280 appearances from 1957 to 1969. He was a member of the Warrington team who won the Lancashire Cup in 1959 and received his certificate from Jackie Edwards. Ken Kelly, my first captain, presented me with my mine. It was a great surprise and great pleasure to be inducted. We joined some cracking players and heroes from the club's past. I say it was a surprise, but I knew something was up early on because Malcolm Lord, who was hosting the dinner, said he would be asking me some questions later. During the interview Malcolm said that if he won the National Lottery the following week he would buy some clothes like mine – and he would only need three balls. Cheeky bugger. In the Lottery, matching three balls wins £25. Every player wishes they could go on forever. But I played for one club for 19 years and 20 seasons – they squeezed in the 1995–96 centenary season before we switched to summer rugby and Super League. Every past player wishes they were playing now and earning the money the players, the full-time players, earn now. But the generation before me – Derek Whitehead, Ken Kelly, Derek Finnigan and Dave Chisnall – all wished they had played in my time because we earned more money than them. The truth is a player has his time and career, be that two, 10 or 20 years, and makes the most of it. And that's what I did. I enjoyed every second and I am still enjoying every second. In the modern game, it will be more difficult to play professionally for 20 years like I did. In future it is going to be difficult to play for 10 years – never mind 20 – because the game is so fast and physical. And great to watch.

Photo: Mark (right) and Alastair Brindle were inducted into the Warrington Wolves Hall of Fame in April 2015. Here they are standing below the Brian Bevan statue at the Halliwell Jones Stadium on the day they were inaugurated. (Photo: Eddie Whitham)

15. Family man

My husband by Gaynor Forster

I have known Mark all my life through our families, but then my mum and dad took over the running of the bars at Wilderspool and Mark and I became good mates. We got engaged in 1985 just before we went to Australia. I was only 19 and Mark was 20. We had an engagement party when we got back and got married in June 1987. Andy Gregory was fantastic as the best man. He looked after me and the bridesmaids, everybody. He even got some ladders to make sure the photographer had a good shot.

Chris was born the following May and everyone thought it was a shotgun wedding, but it wasn't. Mark is a romantic and he loves giving me and the kids surprises. For my 30th birthday he booked a cruise for us and announced it at the kids rugby at Rylands. He just got up on stage and announced it in front of everyone. I went away one weekend and when I got back he had done a full makeover of the back garden, had electricians there and everything. He doesn't show his feelings and the only time I have seen him cry was at my sister Allison's funeral. He is not a great talker either, he likes to keep everything inside, but he is getting better.

Allison had breast cancer at the age of 32 during Mark's first testimonial year. After treatment, she was in remission for six or seven years. Then she got double melanomas on her back. Mark and I went to Las Vegas for our silver wedding anniversary in June 2012 and when we got back she had had a seizure. Our life changed completely because Allison's condition was now terminal. Vegas was now a distant memory because we were concentrating on making sure she got to do all the things on her bucket list, taking her for treatment and, eventually, helping Bernie and Jennie plan her funeral.

Mark and the two boys did the Three Peaks Challenge for charity in her honour. They did it in 24 hours and 20 minutes and so they were just 20 minutes outside their target. Straight from Snowdon Mark had to go to a dinner at a hotel in Bradford to collect an award from BARLA. He could hardly walk. Allison was really poorly that night and we had to take her back to her room. She was 48 when she died in March 2013. It affected Mark a lot because we did everything together and went on holiday together.

I loved watching him play for Warrington every week. I took my dad everywhere and we never missed a game. The only places I didn't go were Fiji, Dubai and America. I had booked flights to go to Milwaukee with my dad, but I was seven months pregnant with Daniel and they wouldn't let me fly. I moved back in with my mum and dad and we paid to listen to the match during the night which my mum wasn't very pleased about because it was very expensive. I didn't like it when he got hurt, but only because I know how much he hates missing rugby. When he got the double sending off in 1991 it was horrendous because of the frustration he felt at not being able to play. He is not a good spectator. I prefer him to play because I know he is enjoying it.

135

Above: Mark with Gaynor and children Beckie, Dan and Chris. Below: Taylor and Maisie, Mark and Gaynor's grandchildren (Photos: courtesy Forster family)

Watching him play for Ireland in the World Cup was fantastic and when he scored that amazing try against New Zealand Maori I ran all the way down the wing with him. He ran around Toa Kohe-Love and will never let him forget it! We are still friends with Toa and Sarah. Mark has never changed. Before a game he didn't get ratty. He switched on when he got to Wilderspool and he switched off when he left the dressing room after the match. Some of the players' wives were dreading it after Warrington got beat because their husbands would be in a foul mood. They would sulk and sulk. Mark always said, after the match, he had tried his best and couldn't do anything about it now so why take it out on your family?

Everyone says to me now "Why don't you make him pack in" but I say why should I stop Mark doing something he loves. He always wanted to play with his lads and he has achieved that. I am sure he would like to play with his grandson Taylor as well. God knows when he is going to hang his boots up.

My Dad by Chris Forster

I was born in May 1988 and I have seen the photos of me going to Wembley in 1990 when I was nearly two, with a flat cap on. Then, when I went to school, all my mates kept asking me if my dad could sign something for them. There would be a knock at the door and mum would say "Your mates are here" and when I opened the door it would be kids asking for my dad's autograph. When I moved from Great Sankey School to Woolston on the first day when I sat down everyone just swarmed around me because my dad played for Warrington.

We went to all the games and we used to drive to Wilderspool in the car and dad would always have Tracy Chapman on or sometimes The Fugees. They were his two favourite pre-match songs he would play on the way. I remember going in the changing rooms after matches and carrying his kit bag out thinking it was the best thing in the world. Just being proud of him really. I wish I had been a little bit older so that I could have enjoyed it more.

I got to know all the players, especially Lee Briers and his partner Vicky, who spent a lot of time at our house. I used to spend a lot of time with the other players' kids on match days. It was like a crèche. I was the mascot at Bradford one year and I remember my dad's testimonial match when Dan, Beckie and I were all mascots, wearing special shirts with "Dad" on the back. We have still got them. It was brilliant at Widnes as well. He went to Widnes with one thing in mind, to get them into Super League, and that's what he did.

I started playing myself when I was aged three, being coached by Kevin Tamati on Bank Park, and it has been in my blood ever since. I played at Rylands Sharks all my junior level from the age of six to under–18s as a half-back. I never wanted to be a winger like my dad. He had the pace, Dan had the tackling and I had the brains and the kicking. If you could put us all together we would have been the best player in the world. I was with Warrington at scholarship level, but my defence let me down and they released me when I was 16. I played for Ireland under–18s in France in the European Championship. They gave me a CD with the national anthem on for us to learn, but I already knew it because my dad had played for them.

I also played for the Great Britain under–18s in Serbia and against the Australian Schoolboys at Whitehaven on a freezing Wednesday night; my mum, dad and granddad came to watch me. Chris Sandow, Israel Folau and Chris Lawrence were in the Australian team. I played scrum-half for Great Britain and Chris Sandow played scrum-half for Australia and he was unbelievably good. He stood out from the rest. He took the whole team on on his own. We knew he was going to be a good player. They beat us 52–6, but I scored our try, kicked our goal and was our man-of-the-match.

I was the BARLA youth player of the year in 2007. Then I got a phone call from John Stankevitch, the Doncaster coach, saying their half-back had done his knee and could I go down to training with them. I panicked and asked if I could ring him back in 10 minutes. I rang my dad and, tight as he is, he said make sure you get your petrol money! I trained on the Thursday night and played Halifax at home on the Sunday. My dad was made up and all the family came to watch me play. My dad was always there to give me advice. He always made sure I was prepared for games, having an early night, eating the right things and he was obsessed with my toe nails, making sure they were cut right because I was the kicker and if my boot was uncomfortable it would affect my game. That's why he is still playing now, because he looked after himself.

I was at Doncaster for the rest of the season and then I signed for Rochdale Hornets under Bobbie Goulding and had a year and a half there. Bobbie was a tough coach for me, as a half-back, because he was a half-back and had done everything in that position. He went on to coach France and knew his stuff. At Championship level I was never going to beat anything Bobbie had done, but it spurred me on, although sometimes I wished I played in the forwards. In one game I scored a hat-trick and was man-of-the-match and he still dragged me into the office and said I could improve on that performance. I just had to nod my head and get on with it.

I went on loan to Blackpool, under Martin Crompton, who was a good friend of my dad's. Martin was a brilliant coach and why he hasn't gone on and got another job in the professional game is beyond me. He was fantastic. But then I did my knee and needed a full knee reconstruction. I tried to come back from that, but injured the knee again and that was it for playing at that level. I went back to playing as an amateur and it was the best thing that could have happened to me because I got to play with my dad and my brother in the same team. Every single game was something to be proud of.

We won quite a few trophies at Bank Quay, including the Lancashire Cup against Widnes West Bank at Leigh Miners. Playing every game with my dad and my brother was good, but especially the finals and winning trophies. I think we won the league that year as well and got to the semi-finals of the National Cup. I honestly don't know how he does it. I am 27 and in bits and he's 50. He is so consistent. I won't be playing at that age. It is weird because you are shouting "Dad" on the field and everyone in the opposition is giving me funny looks and thinking who is he shouting dad to? He doesn't look old enough to be my dad because he is still going strong. He started on the wing, but has slowly worked his way into the centre, second row and, finally, prop. He can't go any further in now.

He played with Dan for Woolston Rovers 'A' against Latchford Albion in the Alliance Cup final in October 2015 – aged 50 – and played for 70 minutes out of the 80 and was making two drives every set. He and my brother both played really well. People in the crowd were asking "How does he do it?" People ask me that every single week and I just say I don't know. My son, Taylor, who was five, was the mascot and walked on to the field with my dad so that was another proud moment. Taylor is already playing football and rugby for Woolston. All my lie-ins have gone now because it is football on a Saturday and rugby on a Sunday. Taylor scored a hat-trick of tries in his first game, which cost me a fortune, and, of course, my dad was there to watch him. When Taylor was in nursery school at the age of two we were called in and the teacher said he was rugby tackling all the kids. I had to explain that we weren't teaching him that, but it came from watching his dad, his uncle and his granddad playing rugby at the weekend. I think he has rugby in his blood as well.

My Dad by Dan Forster

I was born in August 1989 and we used to watch dad every week from the Brian Bevan Stand in the comfy seats. I could see all my mates stood up at the bottom. After the match we went into the Touchdown Club and, after a while, the doors would open and all the fans would come in. Chris and I would carry his kit bag and then play rugby ourselves outside the changing rooms. I started playing properly when I was about seven and played a year above with Chris to make it easier for my mum and dad to watch us. I wasn't fast enough to be a winger, so I played hooker.

I was asked to join the Warrington Wolves scholarship programme at William Beamont High School with Matty Blythe, Mike Cooper and Lee Mitchell, but I had only been at Woolston High School for 18 months and made new mates and didn't want to leave. I played open age at Rylands when I was 16 and was captain of the under–18s in the National Conference League which was a very tough league. So I was playing Saturday and Sunday for four years and then I played in the summer for the likes of Lymm and Crewe. So it was four years non-stop from 16 to 20.

I had the chance to join Rochdale when Chris was there. I went down to training with their under–21s after work, but it wasn't really for me. I was working from seven in the morning until four. Then I was getting changed and travelling to Rochdale, training until eight and then coming home. I was doing that two or three times a week. I didn't have a life and, in the end, I decided I would rather play for fun than pursue a pro career. I knew from day one that it wasn't for me. I would rather have a social life and play with my mates.

I went to Bank Quay Bulls with my dad and Chris, but I broke my leg and was out for eight months. Then I came back and broke my arm. I have been more injured than playing. It's just the way I play to be honest. Playing together with them is weird because the ball goes from me at nine, to Chris at six or seven and he passes it on to my dad in the centre or second row. It is a weird experience. I have never played against a family like that. Even at 50 he is still worth his place in the team. I have been helping out with the coaching and it is hard for me to tell my dad, with all his experience, what to do. I can't tell him off for missing a tackle because he would turn around and shout at me!

We were both playing for Woolston Rovers 'A' against Latchford Albion in the Alliance Cup final in October 2015 and I was brought off with 25 minutes left. Dad was propping and blowing a bit, but he turned around to me as I left the field and said "I'm not coming off" and I couldn't argue with him. He wants to do everything and take as many drives and make as many tackles as he can. Some of the opposition don't like the fact he is a former pro and try to take him out of the game as a bit of a trophy, especially when it is a local derby. I try to look after my dad, but he is old enough and wise enough to look after himself, me and Chris put together. I think he is finally starting to feel his age. When he plays on a Saturday, he can't walk till Wednesday. Then he trains on a Thursday and plays again on Saturday. It is taking its toll.

At training his experience helps all the lads. I am 26 and still learning. He takes the wingers, the centres and the full-back and teaches them what he has learnt in the game. He has given me lots of advice over the years too, not to lose my head basically, because I am a bit of a hothead when I play. He just pulls me to one side and tells me to calm down.

On a Saturday now my daughter Maisie, who is three, comes to watch me play, like I used to watch my dad. Life has come full circle. She is on the sidelines shouting "Dad", "Granddad" and "Uncle Chris" at the same time. It is strange for everyone. She enjoys it, but she will never be putting a pair of boots on. She is going to be doing ballet or something like. She is not going to be playing for Woolston Wildcats. I am putting my foot down from day one. I don't want to see my daughter getting smashed around a rugby field like we do.

My Dad by Beckie Forster

I was born in 1995 and went to my first match when I was two weeks old. By the time I was about four I realised that I couldn't go on a normal day out, especially to Warrington town centre, with my dad because he gets stopped that many times. He will be in a conversation for an hour. Nine times out of 10 I ask him "Who was that dad?" and he says "I don't know". I can go to town and do my shopping and he is still talking to the same person. I refuse to go to town with him now. I never fancied playing rugby and my mum wouldn't let me anyway. I was into dancing, but I probably had to sacrifice that because the boys went training and playing. My friends at school had a girls' rugby team, but it wasn't for me. I did sport at school – netball, canoeing, trampolining and rounders – but rugby was never my thing. I have seen the injuries they suffer and my dad now, still playing at 50, can't walk for a week after and both my brothers have been in the wars. I tell him every week to pack in, but he says he wants to finish on a high.

My school friends thought it was really cool to have a Warrington player as a dad and they all said "Your dad's so good looking". When I started Woolston High School, Daniel was just leaving. PlayStations were popular and there was a rugby league game with my dad on it. The boys in my class all played and thought it was dead good. I was like so what. To this day people ring up when he is on the radio and ask "Are you listening to your dad?" and I say "No, I couldn't think of anything worse. I hear him shouting at me seven days a week. I couldn't think of anything worse than getting in the car, turning the radio on and listening to my dad's voice."

He has always encouraged me to do what I want, but when I was 13 and wanted to go to Africa to do some charity work, without mum and dad, he wasn't a big fan of that but he has got used to it. He has realised now that if I have got something in my mind I am going to do it. My dad is like that himself. I wouldn't say he has spoiled me because I am the only girl, but my brothers would. We all got our equal share and we didn't really get spoiled. My mum's attitude was that just because we had some money it didn't mean that we had to get what we wanted straightaway. We had to wait for Christmas and birthdays like everyone else. People at school couldn't understand that, but we thank mum and dad for that now because we have grown up to know the concept of money. We could easily have been spoilt brats. I remember dad's testimonial match, but only because I hated Wolfie, the Warrington mascot, at the time. I couldn't stand him. Christopher and I had a phobia of things dressed up. Daniel would have loved to have gone to Disney World, but we couldn't because Christopher and I hated people dressed up in costumes. I think Wolfie was more scary then. He looks more friendly now.

(All written in October 2015)

141

Appendix: Statistics and Records

Mark Forster's career in summary

	Apps	Tries	Goals	Pts
Warrington	442+16	191	3	769
Widnes	13+4	3	0	12
Great Britain	2	1	0	4
Ireland	9	5	0	20
Lancs	2	0	0	0
Great Britain Under-21	3	1	0	4
Totals	**471+20**	**201**	**3**	**809**

Mark Forster's Warrington career in summary

Season	Apps	Tries	Goals	Pts
1982–83	2	1	0	3
1983–84	21	8	0	32
1984–85	27+1	16	0	64
1985–86	34+6	14	0	56
1986–87	27+1	10	0	40
1987–88	22+1	8	1	34
1988–89	16	5	0	20
1989–90	35+1	15*	0	60
1990–91	15	6	0	24
1991–92	9+1	5	2	24
1992–93	24+4	6	0	24
1993–94	32	12	0	48
1994–95	40+	24*	0	96
1995–96	18	10	0	40
1996	24+	7	0	28
1997	28	12	0	48
1998	23	11*	0	44
1999	31+1	16	0	64
2000	14	5	0	20
Totals	**442+16**	**191**	**3**	**769**

*indicates the three seasons when Mark Forster was Warrington's leading try-scorer
+ indicates the two seasons when Mark Forster played in every game
Mark Forster made 72 consecutive appearances from 28 December 1993 to 26 November 1995.
Mark Forster also played in seven Locker Cup pre-season 'friendlies' against Wigan, scoring eight tries and receiving the Ernie Ashcroft Shield as man-of-the-match in 1989.

Mark Forster's Warrington appearances: club by club

Club	Appearances		Club	Appearances
Wigan	43+2 as sub		Fulham	1
St Helens	36+1		Dewsbury	1
Bradford	30+1		Rochdale H	1
Castleford	29+1		Runcorn	1
Halifax	29		Trafford Borough	1
Leeds	28+1		Whitehaven	1
Salford	26+1		**Totals**	**442+16**
Hull	23+1			
Oldham	22+2			
Sheffield Eagles	20+1			
Widnes	20+1			
Featherstone	19			
Wakefield	14+1			
Leigh	13			
London Broncos	11			
Hull KR	10+2			
Workington	9			
Huddersfield	7			
Barrow	6+1			
Swinton	5			
Hunslet	4			
Paris SG	4			
York	4			
Doncaster	3			
Gateshead	3			
Blackpool Borough	2			
Carlisle	2			
Keighley	2			
Auckland W	2			
Cronulla	2			
Penrith	2			
Auckland	1			
Australia	1			
Batley	1			
Blackpool Gladiators	1			
Bramley	1			
Chorley Borough	1			

Mark Forster's Warrington tries: club by club

Club	Tries
Wigan	17
St Helens	15
Hull	13
Leeds	11
Salford	11
Bradford	10
Oldham	10
Halifax	9
Wakefield	9
Widnes	9
Hull KR	8
Barrow	7
Workington	7
Featherstone	6
London Broncos	6
Leigh	5
Sheffield Eagles	5
Castleford	4
Doncaster	4
Huddersfield	3
Swinton	3
Blackpool Borough	2
Dewsbury	2
Fulham	2
Gateshead Thunder	2
Paris St Germain	2
Penrith Panthers	2
Auckland Warriors	1
Blackpool Gladiators	1
Bramley	1
Chorley Borough	1
Hunslet	1
Keighley	1
Trafford Borough	1
Total	**191**

Where Mark Forster scored his Warrington tries

Ground	Number of tries
Wilderspool	101
Knowsley Road, St Helens	10
Central Park, Wigan	9
Belle Vue, Wakefield	7
Naughton Park, Widnes	6
The Willows, Salford	6
Headingley, Leeds	5
KC Stadium, Hull	4
Odsal Stadium, Bradford	4
Derwent Park, Workington	3
McAlpine Stadium, Huddersfield	3
Chiswick Polytechnic (Fulham)	2
Don Valley, Sheffield	2
Hilton Park, Leigh	2
Owlerton, Sheffield	2
Stade Saint-Leon, Bayonne	2
Tattersfield, Doncaster	2
The Boulevard, Hull	2
The Stoop, Twickenham	2
Thrum Hall, Halifax	2
Wheldon Road, Castleford	2
Borough Park, Blackpool	1
Bramall Lane, Sheffield	1
Burnden Park, Bolton	1
Craven Park, Hull (old)	1
Craven Park, Hull (new)	1
Elland Road, Leeds	1
Lawkholme Lane, Keighley	1
Penrith Stadium, Penrith	1
Station Road, Swinton	1
South Leeds Stadium, Hunslet	1
The Shay, Halifax	1
Victory Park, Chorley	1
Watersheddings, Oldham	1
Total	**191**

Mark Forster's tries by competition

Competition	Tries
League / Super League	141
John Player / Regal Trophy	17
Challenge Cup	15
Lancashire Cup	9
Premiership Trophy	6
World Club Challenge	3
Total	**191**

Record try-scorers at Wilderspool

	Name	Tries
1	Brian Bevan	464
2	Jack Fish	119
3	John Bevan	112
4	Mark Forster	101

Players with more than 400 appearances for Warrington

	Name	Appearances
1	Brian Bevan	620
2	Parry Gordon	528 plus 15 as a sub
3	Jack Miller	526
4	Mark Forster	442 plus 16 as a sub
5	Gerry Helme	442
6	Jimmy Tranter	439
7	Billy Cunliffe	438
8	Lee Briers	409 plus 14 as a sub
9	Alf Boardman	403

Players with more than 150 tries for Warrington

	Name	Tries
1	Brian Bevan	740
2	Jack Fish	214
3	John Bevan	201
4	Mark Forster	191
5	Parry Gordon & Albert Naughton	167
7	Billy Dingsdale & Lee Briers	154

Where Mark Forster played for Warrington

Position	Appearances
Right wing	156
Right centre	19
Left centre	26
Left wing	240
Stand-off	1
Substitute	16
Total	**458**

Mark Forster's try-scoring feats with Warrington

Four tries in a match (twice)
versus Barrow, John Player Trophy, Wilderspool, 1 December 1985
versus Wakefield, league, away, 12 November 1994

Three tries in a match (five times)
versus Salford, league, Wilderspool, 21 September 1986
versus Leeds, league, Wilderspool, 9 January 1994
versus St Helens, league, Wilderspool, 24 August 1994
versus London Broncos, league, Wilderspool, 20 August 1995
versus Featherstone Rovers, Challenge Cup, Wilderspool, 14 February 1999
Two tries in a match (22 times)
One try in a match (124 times)
Scored tries in 153 matches
Also played in another 305 matches

Mark Forster's winners' medals
Premiership Trophy 1985–86
British Coal Nines 1988–89
Lancashire Cup 1989–90
Regal Trophy 1990–91

Warrington Wolves Hall of Fame
Jack Arkwright (Snr), Kevin Ashcroft, Willie Aspinall, Harry Bath, Brian Bevan, John Bevan, Alf Boardman, Brian Brady, Alastair Brindle, Ernie Brookes, Jim Challinor, Dave Chisnall, Billy Cunliffe, George Dickenson, Billy Dingsdale, Ronnie Duane, Bob Eccles, Jackie Edwards, Jim Featherstone, Jackie Fish, **Mark Forster**, Eric Fraser, Albert Johnson, Laurie Gilfedder, Parry Gordon, Bobby Greenough, Mike Gregory, Jackie Hamblett (Honorary), Gerry Helme, Billy Holding, Ken Kelly, Tommy Martyn, Jack Miller, Alex Murphy, Albert Naughton, Mike Nicholas, Harold Palin, Alf Peacock, Ray Price, Bob Ryan, Bill Shankland, Frank Shugars, Arthur Skelhorn, George Thomas, Tommy Thompson, Jim Tranter, Bobby Wanbon, Derek Whitehead.

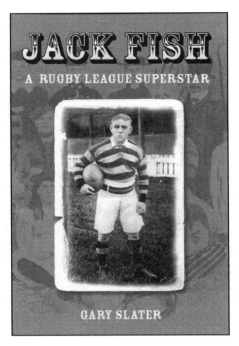

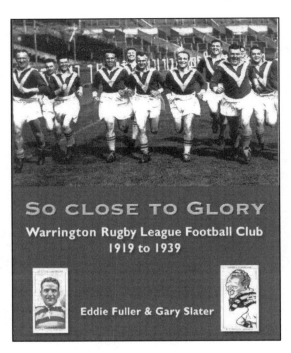

Jack Fish was one of Rugby League's superstars in the sport's early years. He was signed by Warrington in 1898, and soon established himself in the first team. He played in four Challenge Cup Finals, and scored both tries when Warrington beat Hull KR 6–0 in 1905. He captained the team in 1907 when they beat Oldham 17–3 in the Final.

As well as playing 321 games for Warrington, he made 16 appearances for Lancashire and was capped three times by England. He scored a phenomenal 215 tries and kicked 262 goals for the Wire. He is still the only player to score 200 tries and kick 200 goals for Warrington. He coached the Warrington team that reached the 1928 Challenge Cup Final and lived in the town until his death in 1940. This authorised biography is a comprehensive record of Warrington's first superstar. It also provides a vivid portrait of the club's early years in the Northern Union.

Big Jack Arkwright, Jack 'Cod' Miller, Tommy 'Tubby' Thompson, Billy Dingsdale and Bill Shankland are rugby league legends. All five made their names at Wilderspool and are now founder members of the Warrington Wolves Hall of Fame.

So close to Glory is the story of how they and their team-mates in the club's famous primrose and blue colours helped the club to grow in size and popularity during the 1920s and 1930s. In this period the team played in three Challenge Cup Finals and three Championship Finals.

This was a time of poverty, economic hardship and mass unemployment, but Warrington RLFC became a focal point for the town and prospered.

Wilderspool was transformed into a magnificent stadium, the club gained a reputation for signing top-quality Australian players, broke the world record transfer fee and even signed a player from Manchester United. This is the untold story of those two decades and is lavishly illustrated with photographs, cartoons, caricatures and cigarette cards from the period.

Both books are available from London League Publications Ltd: Jack Fish for just £9.95 post free in the UK and So Close to Glory at just £10. Visit www.llpshop.co.uk to order or write to London League Publications Ltd, PO Box 65784 London NW2 9NS

FROM SWN-Y-MOR TO SEATTLE

NICKO'S RUGBY ODYSSEY

MIKE NICHOLAS
WITH GARY SLATER

Mike Nicholas has spent a lifetime in rugby. A boyhood Aberavon fan, he stood on the terraces with Richard Burton before captaining his school's rugby union team as they remained unbeaten for three years. He then played for Aberavon Boys' Club, Aberavon Harlequins and Aberavon Green Stars as a muscular scrum-half. Eventually, he took the Aberavon team by storm as a wing forward and was voted their player of the year for the 1969–70 season.

Tantalisingly close to a Welsh rugby union cap, he turned professional in rugby league in 1972 when he signed for Alex Murphy's Warrington. Two Wembley finals in two years followed as he quickly adapted to the 13-a-side code as a second-row forward.

Denied the chance to play for Great Britain by injury, Mike changed his style of play from running forward to ruthless enforcer, with controversial results. Never sent off in rugby union, he experienced 15 'early baths' in rugby league to become a legend of the northern game. He also played for Wales, including in the 1975 World Championship, later became the team manager and, finally, become president of the Welsh Rugby League.

In 2012, he was inducted on to the Rugby Football League's Roll of Honour for outstanding service to the game. This is the fascinating autobiography of one of rugby league's great characters. All followers of the game will enjoy it.

Available from London League Publications Ltd for just £14. Visit www.llpshop.co.uk to order or write to London League Publications Ltd, PO Box 65784 London NW2 9NS. Cheques payable to London League Publications Ltd.

The book can also be ordered from any bookshop at £14.95

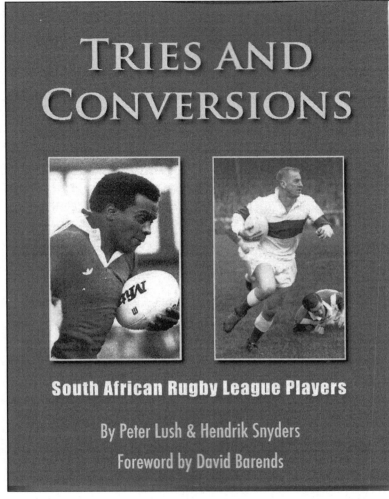

TRIES AND CONVERSIONS

South African Rugby League Players

By Peter Lush & Hendrik Snyders

Foreword by David Barends

In 1910, James Megson and William Mart became the first native-born South Africans to sign for British rugby league clubs. Since then, South African players have made a significant contribution to rugby league.

This book is the first comprehensive study of their contribution to rugby league. It covers players who played in Great Britain and Australia. Some were very successful, such as Attie van Heerden and George van Rooyen in the 1920s, Tom van Vollenhoven in the 1950s and 1960s, and Mark Johnson and Jamie Bloem in the Super League era. But there were also players who never made it after switching codes to play rugby league, and their stories are also told here.

It also includes the players involved in the development of rugby league in South Africa in the early 1960s, the Rugby League Springboks tour of Australia and New Zealand in 1963, and South Africa's participation in the 1995 and 2000 World Cups.

It will be of interest to all rugby followers of both codes, and readers interested in the international development of sport.

Available from London League Publications Ltd for just £14. Visit www.llpshop.co.uk to order or write to London League Publications Ltd, PO Box 65784 London NW2 9NS. Cheques payable to London League Publications Ltd.

The book can also be ordered from any bookshop at £14.95

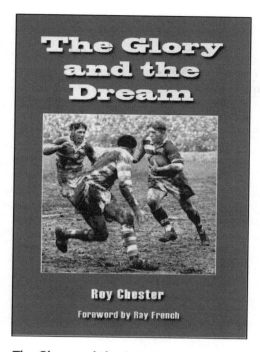

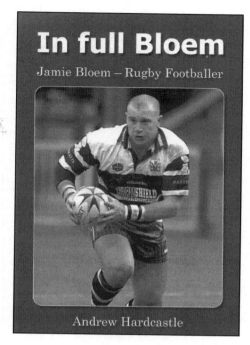

The Glory and the Dream is a great new rugby league novel. It tells the story of a young boy's rite of passage. It is full of rich characters, and is played out against a backdrop of social upheaval in the austere post-war years of rationing and shortages. But it was a time when communities pulled together. Walking days, royal visits, Sunday School outings to the seaside and communal bonfire nights were annual highlights. It was a time when youngsters had to make their own entertainment, including playing rugby league. It is about Johnny Gregson, the young star of the Garton rugby league team, whose dream is to follow his dad's success in the sport. Johnny lives with his mother in Four Locks, a poor working class area in a grimy northern town. His father died in the Second World War. The story starts in 1945, when Johnny is aged 10. It follows his rise from junior rugby league through playing rugby union as a schoolboy to turning professional with Garton.

However, there is much more to Johnny than rugby league. He faces challenges at every turn, including when he wins a scholarship to a local public school and is labelled as a 'slum kid;' by the class bully. His prowess at rugby helps him deal with this boy. Also, at the tender age of 16, he meets a young woman who becomes very important to him. This is a story about sport, romance and working class life. It includes many humorous incidents, insights and even tragedy in a young man's development.

Published in March 2014 at £9.95. **Order for just £6.95 post free in the UK** from www.llpshop.co.uk or by post from London League Publications Ltd, PO Box 65784, London NW2 9NS

In full Bloem is an authorised biography of Jamie Bloem. From being a young South African rugby union player, he developed into a star rugby league player. From 1992 to 2005 he played every position on the field in a career that took in Castleford, Oldham, Doncaster, Widnes and Huddersfield, but primarily Halifax. He later became a coach, commentator and Grade 1 referee. He was never far from the headlines, be it for drug taking, an accusation of biting, charges of abusing referees, declining pay cuts, or even sometimes for scoring spectacular tries or kicking touchline goals. This is a frank account of when he was in the wrong and when he was not. Published in 2013 as a hardback @ £14.95, now available direct from London League Publications Ltd at www.llpshop.co.uk for **just £8.95 post free in the UK** or by post from London League Publications Ltd, PO Box 65784, London NW2 9NS.

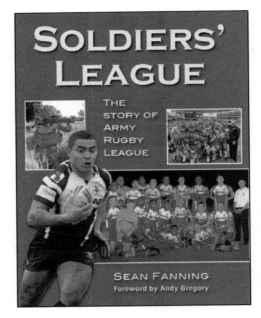

Maurice Oldroyd was one of the key people involved in the development of amateur rugby league since the foundation of the British Amateur Rugby League Association (BARLA) in 1973.

He was the Association's first full-time employee, and played a major role in its development until his retirement in 2000. However, he then became the Association's chairman from 2001 to 2005, and today is the Association's patron.

This fascinating memoir reflects on his life and involvement in rugby league. Maurice Oldroyd has been at the centre of amateur rugby league since 1973. This well- illustrated, fascinating memoir is essential reading for all rugby league fans.

Published at £12.95, available for **just £5.00 post free in the UK** from www.llpshop.co.uk or by post from London League Publications Ltd, PO Box 65784, London NW2 9NS.

Rugby league only became a recognised sport in the Army in 1994. However, since then it has thrived, overcoming many obstacles on the way. This book is the first to be published about rugby league in the Armed Forces. It covers the growth and development of the sport, including: Inter-Services matches; The Army in the Challenge Cup; International matches and tours; The Lawson and Yeoman Cups; Combined Services rugby league; Profiles of players, coaches, managers and officials; Rugby league and the Army prior to 1994; and a tribute to Jack Harrison, the only professional rugby league player to win the Victoria Cross who was playing when he enlisted.

Sean Fanning played professional rugby league for Leigh and Highfield. He was a Staff Sergeant in the Army Medical Service until 2014, and was on active duty in Afghanistan in 2012. He has played for and coached the Army Rugby League team, played for the Great Britain Armed Forces team in the 2008 Armed Forces World Cup and has played for Combined Services. His share of the profits from this book will be paid directly to Soldiers' League, which raises money for service charities, including the Royal British Legion, Blesma and Combat Stress.

Published in 2013 @ £14.95, now available direct from London League Publications Ltd at www.llpshop.co.uk for **just £14.00** (£10 for current or serving members of the Armed Forces) post free in the UK or by post from London League Publications Ltd, PO Box 65784, London NW2 9NS.